Spearman to Minuteman

Spearman to Minuteman

The Story of the Soldier
2000 B.C.—1783 A.D.

S. E. Ellacott

Abelard-Schuman
LONDON
NEW YORK
TORONTO

BY THE SAME AUTHOR

THE NORMAN INVASION

CONSCRIPTS ON THE MARCH: The Story of the Soldier,
from Napoleon to the Nuclear Age

LONDON
Abelard-Schuman
Limited
8 King Street WC2

NEW YORK
Abelard-Schuman
Limited
257 Park Avenue South

TORONTO
Abelard-Schuman
Canada Limited
1680 Midland Avenue
Scarborough

Contents

Illustrations

Introduction

There is no story as intriguing as that of the old-time soldier—the man behind the shield, on the charging horse, or serving, his face blackened by powder, at the high-wheeled cannon. He was the typical figure of the armies of former days—the professional, volunteer soldier whose career was war. This is the story not of the great generals, but of the ordinary fighting men who won the victories of the Egyptian kings, and made up the ranks of the Spartans at Thermopylae. It tells of the military machine of the Romans, and the ranked bowmen of the Middle Ages, and how all were hammered into effective military formations. All had to be fed, clothed and armed, taught skill in arms and controlled movement in steadfast units.

Among European armies, the military efficiency of the 18th-century Prussians became the model. The story of its application to the Continental Army of George Washington concludes this book. Life in the armies of the 19th and 20th centuries is depicted in another book by the same author, *Conscripts on the March: The Story of the Soldier from Napoleon to the Nuclear Age*; the era in which the typical soldier was an amateur; a tiny part of the nation in arms.

1. Genesis

High and clear the trumpet note, winging through the blazing heat. Across the wide drill ground there was a precise, ordered movement as the advancing battalion deployed into line. No sound attended the men's progress, for the thick, red dust, rolling in clouds around their feet, muffled the pad-pad of sandals.

Here was no unit of the 20th century, despite the military bearing and the regulated pace. Well over three thousand years ago these well-disciplined troops served in the army of the Egyptian king. Egypt then led the ancient world by her command of the first fighting force wherein the men were trained to respond, machinelike, to the sound of trumpet or drum. These soldiers who stepped in rigid line across the drill ground were heavy infantry—double-armed men, each with copperheaded axe and spear. The

DISCIPLINED TROOPS
EGYPT, 1450 BC.
Based on wall-pictures: Thebes.

latter was held upward at an angle, while the squarish, round-topped shield was braced upon the arm. This form of shield was framed in wood and covered with bull's hide, copper-studded. There was a grip, either transverse or vertical, inside the shield, and in some cases it was slung by a leather strap.

Among Egyptian men a close felt cap was commonly worn, to keep off the fierce rays of the sun, so the helmet of the soldier was of the same form. It was made in a series

[12]

of quilted divisions, to give added protection, and body armour was provided by gluing together layers of flax.

Another form of protection sometimes worn by infantry was a kind of shirt with overlapping metal scales, shaped like an Egyptian shield. Below the body armour was the kiltlike garment of everyday life. This was a piece of linen about six feet long, with one edge straight and the other curved, forming a point at each end. At its widest part, the strip measured about eighteen inches across.

The wearer put on the kilt with the straight edge upward, passing one point across the midriff and around the right hip. He then brought the remainder around the back, carrying it forward over the right hip to the middle of his body. There the point was turned in over the straight edge or brought up underneath to hang over. In either case, the point was pulled down to hang before the legs, a girdle being knotted around the waist to secure the garment.

Hardy fellows, these spearmen. Their skin was burned dark and their wiry bodies toughened by rigorous early training, like every soldier of the Pharaoh. An able-bodied boy whose father was in the army had to become a soldier; it was forbidden for him to follow any other profession. Army life was begun at twelve, and at fifteen the young cadets were already inured to the long day of physical exercises, marching, and battle training.

Bodily fitness was highly regarded among soldiers, so that wrestling, leaping, and mock combat with cudgels were popular amusements. It was common for men in training to run several miles each morning before breakfast.

At night there was the plank bed with scanty covering, and the daily meals were chiefly of bread and vegetables, with little meat. It is a curious thing that in Egypt, where the system of large-scale corn-growing was first devised, the great mass of the population saw little of the crop in their diet. Among the peasants the staple food comprised a variety of roots, for the greater part of the corn output went in trade.

It is true that the serving soldier, his initial training over, fared better than the peasant. The former ranked high in the Egyptian hierarchy during the age of conquest, between the 16th century B.C. and the 12th. For instance, the royal guards had five pounds of bread, two pounds of meat, and two pints of wine as their daily rations per man.

Every soldier was given a substantial grant of land, free of tribute, and this land he usually rented out. In this way the income formed his pay, and he had a place of retirement when his army career was over. Farming was regarded as a worthy occupation for a soldier, whereas he would hold in contempt a mechanic's work. Such was the soldier's importance to the state that the civil authorities were not permitted to imprison him for debt. We must remember that all payments were made in goods or by work, as at that time there was no money among the Egyptians.

The empire won by the Egyptian soldier had its beginnings under the Pharaoh Thutmose III, who ruled for about fifty years from 1500 B.C. He was the first great general, and under his direction the small standing army that had been maintained during the earlier years was greatly expanded. A system was devised by which units employing different weapons were trained in co-operation. Some groups were composed of mercenaries, who were paid in goods instead of being awarded land.

The army employed a wide range of weapons, which the recruits provided—bows, slings, spears, short javelins, swords and daggers, axes of different types, maces, and short, curved sticks called in recent times *lissau*. This is an Arabic word meaning "tongue," and it refers to the shape of the weapon. It appears to have been used as a lighter form of the mace; the latter had a thirty-inch shaft with a large ball at the end.

Some of the small axes had straight handles, hooked at the end for hanging in the girdle, while others were curved to give greater force to the blow. All blades were made of copper or bronze, with edges hardened by hammering. A

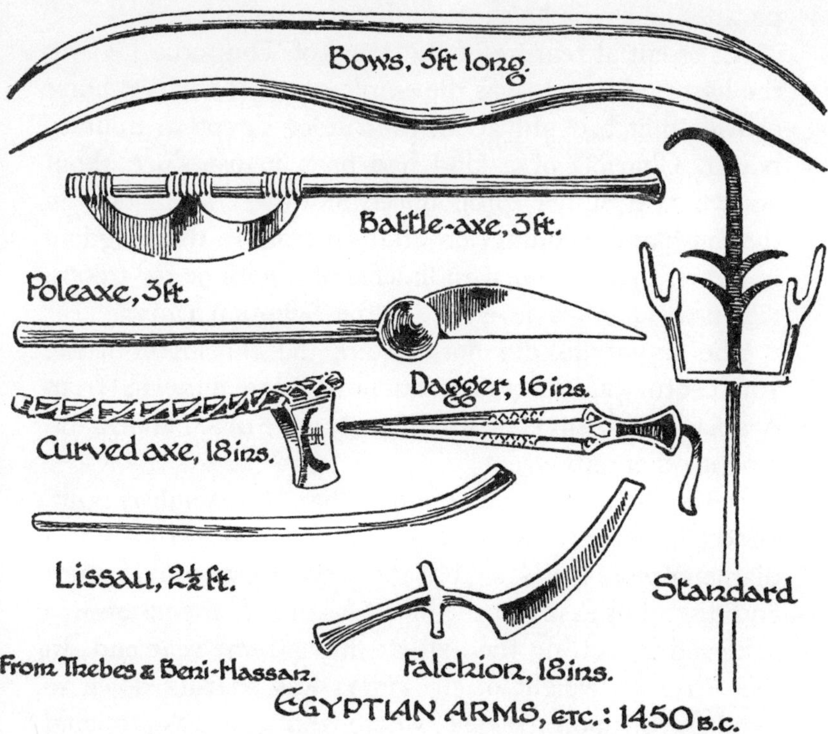

drawback of the personal system of supply was that the Egyptian forces could not have standardized equipment.

There was a high degree of organization in the grouping of infantry into units, like battalions and regiments, with standards. Each standard represented some sacred object or device, and each was borne on a staff or on the point of a spear by an officer chosen for his bravery. Sometimes this officer wore a distinguishing symbol upon his chest. It might show two lions, expressing courage, or flies, which, though repulsed, continually returned to the attack. The Order of the Fly was among the Pharaoh's military decorations for bravery.

There does not appear to have been much difference in the equipment of an officer, except that on ceremonial parades he carried a short staff and no weapons.

An essential feature of the army of Thutmose III was the horse soldier. It was the employment of the two-horse chariot that brought about the rise of Egyptian military power. Chariots of a kind had been in use since about 3000 B.C. in Sumer (pronounced Shu-mer), a kingdom in the south of the country now named Iraq. In this kingdom of Sumer arose the first rudiments of discipline for troops, which was further developed in the Egyptian army.

The Egyptians did not acquire the chariot until the 16th century B.C., and their first horses were imported from Arabia. Later, Egyptian-bred horses were much in demand among other nations.

In the Pharaoh's army the war chariot was lightly built, almost of skeleton form. Low wheels about 30 inches in diameter were fitted, so that the crew of two could mount and dismount easily at the back. A kind of suspension was achieved by setting the axle at the extreme rear end. In this way the weight of the riders was bearing down to some extent upon the pole, whose front end was attached to the yoke over the horses' necks. The open sides of the chariot reached to the riders' thighs, and the front, at the same level, was of a solid triangular form.

On each side, pointing obliquely forward, a flexible bow case was attached, so that each man had a bow at hand. When the bow was withdrawn, the upper part of the case turned down and hung. Usually, when the chariot was in action, the left-hand man drove while the other man shot arrows, but in the thick of the fight the driver lashed the reins around his waist to join in.

In addition to the bow cases, another case was fixed at each side of the chariot. These cases, whose tops pointed to the rear, contained short javelins and a further supply of arrows, to supplement those in the men's quivers and on

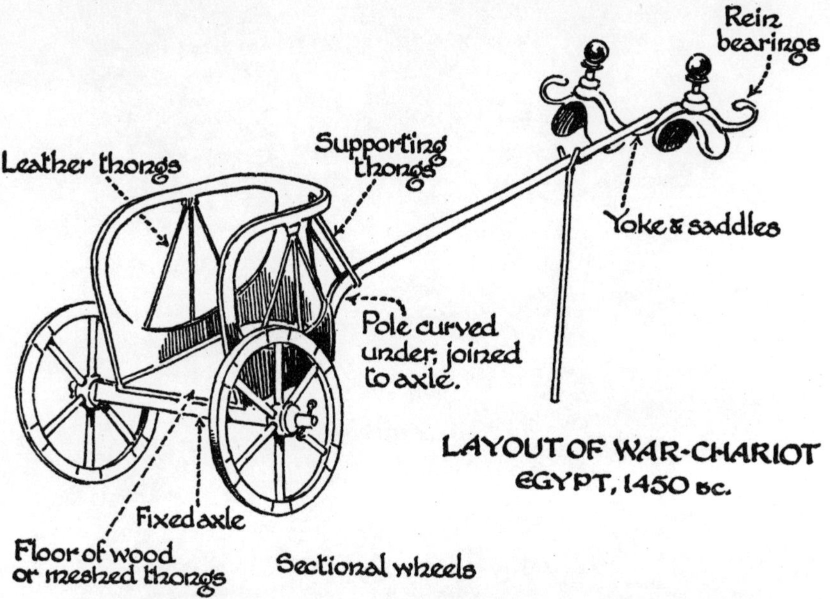

the floor of the vehicle. As already mentioned, the horses were yoked to a central pole, with inside traces; each horse had a girth and a form of martingale. A simple bridle with diverging cheekpieces was provided, and the bit was a plain bar across the tongue. Bearing rings carried the reins from the bridle, and the chariot horses of kings and nobles each mounted a tall plume of feathers. Thutmose III himself is recorded as having a chariot of electrum, a natural mixture of pale gold and silver.

Charioteers in the ranks were required to service their

own vehicles, and it was part of their training to dismantle and reassemble them. Though the vehicles were the same, chariot troops were divided into light and heavy sections. The former simply harassed the enemy with spears and arrows, but the latter, often provided with shields and long lances, were literally shock troops; Egyptian artists

CHARIOTS IN THE CHARGE: EGYPT, 1450 B.C.

often showed them driving straight into the opposing forces. The effect must have been tremendous upon an undisciplined enemy—the long lines of racing horses, the arrow-shower pouring from the advancing ranks, and the smashing impact of scores of hoofs. Occasionally a small group of heroes, or even a single man, would issue a personal challenge to the enemy.

An example of artists' heroics is to be seen in the wall

[18]

picture of Seti I, a 14th-century Pharaoh, in battle. The king appears alone in his chariot, apparently shooting arrows ahead, while his opponents are shown, like pygmies, tumbling in all directions before the rearing horses. We do not assume that the king actually fought alone; the artists did not wish to detract from the dramatic effect by adding another figure in the chariot. Another point was the huge size of the king-figure compared to the enemy; it would have been a problem to decide on the size for the other man.

Though some ancient historians, like Herodotus, have attributed vast armies to the warlike Pharaohs, it is not likely that these exceeded 30,000 men. During the age of conquest, armies like this, archers, horse soldiers, and variously-armed infantry, subjected a number of Asiatic nations. Among the wall pictures of military affairs, nothing is shown in the way of cavalry. In fact, only two pictures show Egyptians on horseback, and those are of the Roman era. However, it seems reasonably certain that the Egyptians used cavalry, probably as a harassing force.

During one expedition of Thutmose III against the Syrians, the Hittite King of Kadesh loosed a mare among the Egyptians' chariots, to excite the stallions and break up the line. However, an astute Egyptian general saw the device and killed the mare.

Another warrior Pharaoh, Rameses II, son of Seti I, had to his credit the first recorded flanking movement, carried out at the same scene of action, Kadesh, on the River Orontes. The Pharaoh's wearied forces were hard pressed when a detached division, called up by urgent message, fell upon the Hittites' rear and routed them.

In preparing for a warlike expedition, the Pharaoh issued a mobilization order to every province, which contributed a set quota of troops. Usually the king took command, though on some occasions a high-ranking general might take the post. Before moving off from the muster, at the place appointed as a general rendezvous, each soldier bowed deeply to the king. He was positioned in his war chariot at the centre point of the march. Chariots were in the lead; next came variously-armed infantry units, who preceded the king, and a strong force of infantry formed the rear-guard.

On the battlefield, the trumpet signal brought a shower of arrows upon the enemy, and a large detachment of heavy charioteeers made a frontal attack. As the spear-armed infantry moved up in close order, supporting light chariots and cavalry kept up constant pressure on the enemy wings. Meanwhile, the archers tried to disorder the centre with the arrow shower.

A creditable feature of the Egyptian soldier was his clemency to the defeated. In an age when this virtue was uncommon, cases of cruelty are not often to be found in Egyptian records. It was customary to cut off the right hands of the enemy dead, in order to count their losses for a report to the Pharaoh. This record of success was acknowledged by a reward that was divided among the whole army.

At the end of a victorious action in the open field, the troops prepared a temporary rectangular camp. In its midst were gathered the prisoners, together with the captured horses, chariots, arms, and other spoils. Prisoners were of great value, to supply the constant demand for slaves in brickmaking, building, and farming. It was this usefulness that caused the disastrous refusal to release the Hebrew slaves at Moses' request.

When the army's action was mounted against a fortified town, the archers were much to the fore. They were employed to keep the enemy from manning his walls, so that the assault troops could get to close quarters. The attackers brought forward huts framed in wood and covered with hides, to allow sappers to undermine the walls while protected from enemy missiles. Sometimes scaling ladders were mounted upon them. Where the fortifications were built on a rock, short spikes of metal were thrust into cracks to help the climbers.

We may well realize that the Egyptians' ascendancy in war was gained by combined ingenuity and skilful organization, quite apart from the physical prowess and courage required. Yet these remarkable people were not truly militaristic. Their spurt of empire building, engendered by the import of horse and chariot, was a phase not really in keeping with their national outlook.

After four centuries, the end of the Egyptian soldier's power came about in a strange way. The young Pharaoh, Amenhotep IV, paved the way for his country's fall during the 14th century B.C., before the time of Seti I. Amenhotep refuted the various Egyptian gods, and declared for a single deity, the Sun-God. A doctrine of peace and the love of beautiful things were features of this faith, which was regarded sourly by the priests of the old gods.

The priests worked to spread discontent in the army, and this was not difficult. Amenhotep's peaceful policy had left the soldiers idle, and a disturbed confusion spread through the ranks.

News of the trouble travelled throughout the Egyptian empire in Asia, and a spirit of revolt flourished. It is true that, when the monotheistic Pharaoh died, a new line of kings made desperate efforts to repair the damage. Seti I and his son Rameses II were outstanding figures in this, but even their personal courage at the head of their troops could not drive the Hittites from the Syrian territory. These Hittites, the great ironworkers of the ancient East, had many iron weapons where the Egyptian soldier was armed with bronze.

Once the great edifice of Egyptian power had been

undermined, nothing could make it sound again. Those drawings at Thebes that depict the later years of the empire show an increasing number of foreign mercenaries in the ranks. King after king revolted to throw off the Egyptian yoke, and by the middle of the 12th century B.C., the enfeebled Egyptian armies were crushed by swarming enemies. The first true soldiers went down before those who had emulated their skill at war.

2. The Nation of Soldiers

While the Egyptian empire was being carved out by the warrior Pharaohs, the stage was set for the entry of the first European soldiers. When they first appeared, the light-skinned sheepherders from the broad pastures of the southern Danube were hardly fit for the rôle.

Three successive waves overran the Aegean territory and occupied the country that we now call Greece. First came the Achaeans, spreading southward to reach the farthest coast, and no doubt they were suitably awed at the sight of the flourishing cities of the Aegean peoples of 1500 B.C. Upon the heels of the Achaeans came their conquerors, the Dorians, who did not stop at the formers' limits. Having learned a little seamanship from the Aegeans, the Dorians occupied the island of Crete, and spread thence to the other islands of the southern Aegean. These invaders were the most powerful of the three races concerned; when the Ionians came, they simply mingled with their predecessors.

Widespread over the mainland of Greece, the strangers intermarried with their unwilling hosts the Aegean peoples, and a series of unconnected settlements grew up. These were groups of villages, each group under a central control, and in time each merged into a single independent city-state.

There was one notable exception, upon which our attention is directed. A group of Dorian families occupied a pleasant valley in the district of Laconia, and they called their settlement Sparta. Their villages, spread over an area about two miles across, were not combined into a city, for the Spartans liked spacious gardens. As the site was inland, the settlers relied upon the surrounding mountains for protection, and Sparta boasted no walls until late in the 4th century B.C.

In these agreeable surroundings grew up the most re-markable people of the ancient world—remarkable for their physical prowess and dogged courage. The Egyptians had given the soldier a high place in their community, but here we see a race of soldiers.

In order to avoid giving one man full powers, two kings maintained joint rule over the nation, with hereditary succession. As the kings were rated like demigods, they were high priests as well. The kings shared a royal palace, and they were the joint leaders of the army in war. Though the Spartans did not habitually seek war—they were not easily roused—for 500 years their armies were a byword throughout Greece.

In addition to the Spartans themselves, two subject peoples lived in the valley. First in importance were the Periœci ("dwellers around the city"), who were the original inhabitants of the district. These people were freemen and landholders, with limited self-government,

but without any voice in state matters. Far below them in status were the Helots, in effect serfs, who were bound to the land of their Spartan owners. Their numbers were chiefly made up of captured Messenians, natives of a bordering state.

Helots paid rent amounting to about half their yearly crops, but at least they lived with their families, and they could not be sold out of the country. Like the mediaeval serfs, Helots owed military service, and men who acquitted

[25]

themselves with notable bravery could gain their freedom.

Among the Spartans, courage, strength, and endurance
were considered the prime virtues. For that reason, racial
purity was a fetish, and sickly or deformed children might
be exposed to die on the hillside. At the age of seven, the
Spartan boy began a course of the severest training in
physical and mental fortitude. He was exposed to dire
hardships, and subjected to extremes of heat and cold,
with a minimum of food. The authorities devised courses
of physical training, which included ceaseless backbreak-
ing work and long, dangerous mountain expeditions.

After five years of this form of early training, the boy
was ready for the pre-manhood tests. These resembled
very much the traditional rites of the North American
Indians, when a youth was tested for admission among
the braves. Spartan tests comprised, in the first place, a
severe whipping. At a public ceremony, each of the young
candidates was lashed with all the force of two men. This
ordeal was witnessed by the boys' mothers, as a test of
their own fortitude. It was understood that if a mother
could no longer endure the sight, she could stop it. In the
same way, her son was free to declare that he could not
go on, but if either caused this check, the boy would be
banned from the army.

Endurance of another kind formed the second great
test. Candidates had to abstain from food and drink for
several days and nights, while living in the open. Watchers
were posted, who ate and drank nearby, with exaggerated
enjoyment, while the most appetizing meals were kept
within reach of the candidates. As before, they were free
to end the ordeal for themselves, but with the same penalty.

A very impressive feature of the whole system was that
all young males, of high or low degree, had to endure the
same treatment. The idea was to achieve a calm steadfast-

ness, unperturbed by any degree of suffering, mental or physical. It was common for youths to compete to be lashed before the altar of Artemis, that their endurance of pain might pay respect to the goddess.

Passivity in acute discomfort was one goal to be attained, but another was ability and self-preservation in war. At intervals, youths in training were sent out to live upon the country—they were required to forage for food, stealing while yet avoiding detection.

Another characteristic to be developed was ruthlessness in obedience to state decrees, and here a brutal form of training was practised. As already mentioned, the Helots were literally slaves, and though they were not ill-used in general, there were occasional stirrings of rebellion among them. For this reason, dagger-armed youths were appointed to carry out the *crypteia*, the annual stealthy killing of a number of Helots, to thin their ranks. A frightful massacre of this kind was perpetrated in 464 B.C., "for the safety of the state", after a violent earthquake.

With this rigorous background, the Spartan soldier attained manhood, his body toughened, his mind indoctrinated with the spirit of service to the state. Around him, the womenfolk of his family were as steadfast in outlook as he was. Women were held in the highest esteem, as actual or potential mothers of Spartan soldiers. While growing up, girls were trained in athletics, to run, wrestle, and box like men. They had to nerve themselves, if need be, to see their weakly children put out to die, and their fine sons bleeding under the lash.

Every Spartan was first and foremost a citizen of the state, and this was well expressed in the great national feature, the *syssitia*, the public meal-taking. Spartan citizen-soldiers were divided into groups of fifteen, and each member provided food from his landholdings. Game and wine came from the public forests and vineyards.

[27]

No soldier could be excused from membership of a mess, and every member had to be present at the meal. Even the kings were thus compelled. By this means the citizens' duty and obedience received a constant reminder.

In this picture of strictly-regulated public life, the accent has been upon physical and mental training, for a good reason. Art and industry played no part in Spartan life. It is true that a little music and poetry were admitted, but the military mind had nothing to do with mechanics and agriculture. Such things were left to the Periœci and the Helots. It was by these people's toil that the Spartan was enabled to lead his home life in hunting and in military exercises.

Though we speak of "a Spartan life" to express a chosen minimum of physical comfort, this really applied to the Spartan in youth. Early training built up the man to such a degree that the physical standards remained, with the ability to endure hardship, but life in general was easier for the trained soldier. His home was pleasant and comfortable, he did no work, and all his needs were provided from his slave-worked land.

These privileges formed the basic pay of the soldier, as his share of the state that he defended. Another source of shared income was the taxes levied upon subject towns, whose townsmen had no votes.

Each succeeding generation of Spartans faithfully carried out the racial traditions, without realizing that such rigidity tended to isolate them in the expanding Greek world. They did colonize southern Italy, in their city of Tarentum, but outside affairs concerned them little. They were disposed to consider Sparta the champion Greek state, and let it rest at that. In fact, during the 6th century B.C. the Spartans had forcibly annexed almost all of the Peloponnese, to form the most powerful state in Greece.

The truly formidable army of the Spartans was an infantry force, with attendant light troops recruited from their subject peoples. Though there was a body of cavalry, it was of little value as a shock unit, and the idea of using it for reconnaissance had not then been conceived.

By reason of their iron nerve and immense physical strength, the Spartans built up a nationwide reputation. In their massive *phalanx*, thousands of *hoplitai* (free citizens) pointed forward the long spear, braced the large round shield before the chest, and moved with measured tread upon the objective.

One may well picture the reaction of the opponents. They would be confronted by that rolling human tide, slowly advancing with its leading edge of glittering points. The fearful knowledge, these are the Spartans—the indecision, while the menacing front bears down upon them —then the impact, cleaving a wide gap as the bare, bronze-greaved legs march ponderously on. Through the scattering enemy ranks rolls the irresistible mass, leaving a broad swathe of destruction. At close quarters, the sword sweeps in, and in grim silence those hard, brown faces, overshadowed by high-crested helmets, pass on. Rank follows rank, trampling the wreck of the opposing forces, and there is no more to do.

In spite of their relative unpopularity among the Greek states, the organization of the Spartans' army was highly regarded. Xenophon (430–354 B.C.) the Athenian militarist, wrote that the army system showed "admirable simplicity in the midst of seeming intricacy." An enlightening comment was made by his fellow countryman Thucydides. The latter showed that the basis of the Spartans' efficiency in this respect was the elaborate grading of authority from the top down, so that a general's orders were quickly and easily transmitted to the ranks.

Though relying upon their steam-roller method of

attack, the Spartans were most cautious when they under-
took an operation. They preferred to conceal their inten-
tions until the last moment. No one could question their
bravery, but they never engaged the enemy needlessly, nor
pursued when it was not necessary for victory. Cowardice
was the unthinkable fault to them. There is some basis to
the story of the Spartan mother saying to her son regarding his shield: "Return with it or on it" (in other words,
alive with unstained reputation, or dead).

The most famous illustration of the stubborn courage of
the Spartan soldier is the action at the Pass of Thermopylae ("hot springs"), at the northern end of the Malian
Gulf. In the summer of 480 B.C., the invader Xerxes of
Persia was nearing the pass with 200,000 men, while an
army of a little over 5,000 Greeks was on its way to the
same point. Leading the defenders was one of the kings of
Sparta, Leonidas ("Son of the Lion").

On his arrival, the king shrewdly weighed his position.
A high, steep cliff bounded the pass on one side, and on
the other there was a sharp drop into the sea. For this
reason, the Persians could only attack on a narrow front,
with a few men abreast. Leonidas accordingly pared down
his forces to suit the cramped defence position. He finally
disposed 300 Spartans in the vanguard, supported by 700
Thespians and a body of Thebans.

There was close and bloody work in that narrow pass
when the Persians came. All day, their frenzied screaming
rose like the cries of sea birds, as the snakehead of the
attackers writhed along the hanging pass, beat itself
against the rigid Spartan wall, and fell back shattered.

In the Persian forces, the archer was supreme, and for
the open field this was a formidable arm. However, this
situation gave little scope for archery, so the attack had to
be man to man. Upon the helmets and breastplates of the
Spartan vanguard the blows had little effect; not so their

own strokes against the lightly-clad attackers. Many feet below, the waves lapping the cliff foot were bright with gaudy trappings, where the fallen Persians washed to and fro.

Here and there the scattered arrows found their mark and sent one of the defenders to join the wrack, but when

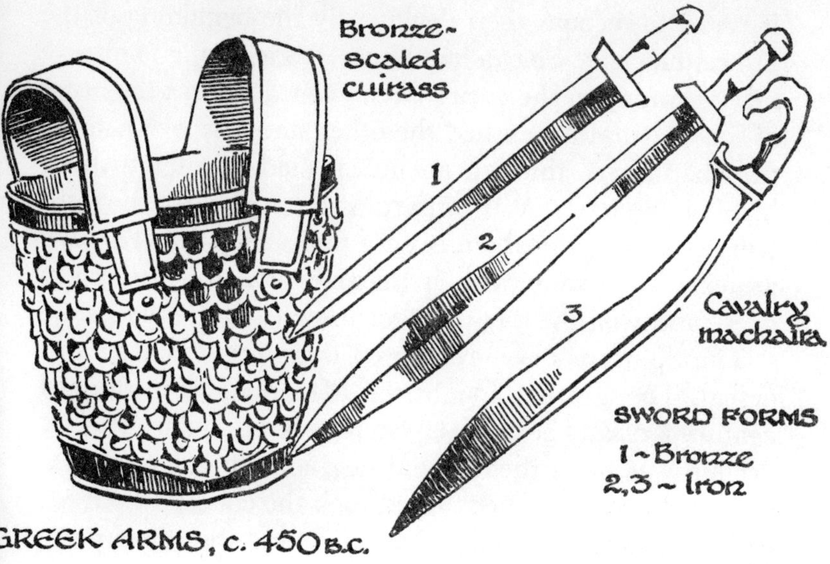

GREEK ARMS, c. 450 B.C.

daylight faded the pass was still in the king's hands. There was some hope that the brawny, sunburned arms, weary with striking, might find a little ease under cover of the dark.

It was at this stage that a catastrophe thundered down on the king. Upon the rear burst a detachment of the enemy. The Greek traitor Ephialtes had led them across the mountains in a flanking movement.

Like trapped wolves, the Spartans sold their lives at a fearful price, and the Thespians backed them nobly. Yet there could be but one end. Leonidas, his Spartans, and their worthy allies were united in a red fellowship of death; the coward Thebans threw down their arms.

Fighting men still remember the soldiers of the Hot Springs. Since that day of slaughter, the pass has changed much. The cliff has been eroded by the weathering of twenty-five centuries, to become sloped and shallow, and the sea has receded many miles. Still, the story lives, and while men bear arms it will not be forgotten.

In spite of the many defects in the Spartans' way of life, it is sad to recount their decline. By the beginning of the 4th century B.C., Sparta had blundered in trying to impose her system upon the entire Greek world. It was the army of Thebes that astonished the other states by overcoming the champions, through an unexpected counter to their hidebound tactics. As the Spartans always fielded the right wing of their army about twenty ranks deep, the Thebans attacked this wing with a massive phalanx fifty ranks deep, and won the day by sheer force (Leuctra, 371 B.C.).

The Spartans never recovered their prestige after this defeat. Though they fought the Macedonians in the 3rd century B.C., and beat off the Epirean King Pyrrhus in 272, decline was upon them. Final degradation came when a robber chieftain, named Nabis, took the country. Sparta's best citizens were killed or banished, and the country became a hive of robbers.

When the Greek soldier-hero Philopoemen purged the state (188 B.C.), he forced the citizens to destroy their walls and accept the Achaean system of government. Surely the mournful shades of departed heroes lamented over the dying valley.

3. Masters of the Inland Sea

Already the Mediterranean world had seen the rise and fall of two great soldier communities. There came then, driving to the fore, the greatest that the world had seen. From small beginnings, humble copying of the Greek trader cities and their forces, the widely flung Roman empire girdled the inland sea. Set up as it was upon the ranks of Roman armies, the empire drew upon the strength and courage of the soldier for its lifeblood.

When the little Roman city-state first built up its forces, early in the 6th century B.C., the army was drawn from the ruling class. Later, under the threat of the surrounding tribes, plebeians were recruited by Servius Tullius, sixth king of Rome, during the 6th century B.C. The richest Romans were given preference. They were fielded as *equites*, mounted infantry, while those next in order of wealth formed the heavy infantry. Plebeians were classed as *rorarii*, light troops.

At first the Romans used the Greek phalanx, in three lengthwise divisions—*principes*, i.e., the chief rank, to bear the first onset; *hastati*, spearmen in the second rank, and *triarii*, older men. Each "rank" consisted of several lines of men.

Infantry arms were the *hasta*, or thrusting spear, a straight, two-edged Greek sword with an obtuse point, and a dagger. The wealthy, mounted men provided their own horses and armour. They wore metal-reinforced corselets, crested helmets, and greaves, and they carried round shields (*clipei*).

These arrangements held good until the time of Camillus (485 B.C.–365 B.C.), a Roman commander of legendary fame. One of the most important reforms credited to Camillus was the division of the three ranks into smaller units known as *maniples*. These comprised from sixty to 120 men, and the object was flexible movement.

During the 5th and 4th centuries B.C., Rome's chief enemies were the Etruscans and the Samnites. Both nations employed a light seven-foot javelin, known to the Romans as a *pilum*. This arm was adopted by the Romans, and was one of the reasons for the breakup of the old solid formation into the *legion* composed of small units. It was awkward to throw spears from closely-packed ranks, so an open order had to be arranged.

In the reformed force, the *hastati* became the front rank and the *principes* the second, each rank divided as *maniples* and armed with *pila*. It seems that the *triarii* in the rear rank maintained the old close order, and still kept the *hasta*.

The second great advance supposedly instituted by Camillus was a system of regular payment for the soldier, though it is difficult to find details of the rate of pay in the 4th century B.C. However, this made possible longer periods of service; the men were no longer obliged to return home, after a short tour of duty, to attend to business or farm affairs. It became possible to carry out a winter campaign, at need.

Between 241 B.C. and 146 B.C., the Roman army fought three major wars (the Punic Wars) with the Phoenician trader-city of Carthage. It stood near the site of present-day Tunis, in north Africa. When Carthage was finally defeated, the Romans had gained a great deal of practical experience in the best means of organizing their forces. A regular annual enlistment was carried out, for raising two armies each two legions strong, to be commanded by two consuls. In each legion there were six military tribunes—representatives of the consuls. These tribunes took turns in selecting men from the year's call-up, to form in the end four legions of at least 4,200 men each.

A man's possessions still determined his position in the army. The youngest and poorest men were enlisted as *velites*, skirmishers. They were armed with the *hasta velitaris*, a light throwing spear just under four feet long, and their protection was a round buckler (*parma*). A regular legion consisted of *velites*, *hastati*, and *principes*, twelve or thirteen hundred of each, and the *triarii*, the oldest men, were never more than 600.

Attached to each legion were 300 cavalry, divided into ten squadrons (*turmae*), each with a *decurion* in charge. The men were armed with lances ten to twelve feet long and the *spatha* or long sword. In most cases they were not

Romans, but men of subject peoples, who had been brought into the army.

When the legion was drawn up in order of battle, during the second Punic War, the old three-rank formation was maintained. In the front rank, the *hastati* were divided into ten maniples, each comprising two "centuries" originally, as the name implies, of a hundred men. Now there were sixty. Between the maniples were spaces equal to the frontage of one maniple. These spaces were covered by the *principes* in the second rank, where a similar disposition was made. At that time (the end of the 3rd century B.C.) the *triarii* in the rear rank were organized in maniples of one century, which covered the spaces in the second rank. Men were always allocated to the rank suited to their age and fitness; wealth was not now the deciding factor.

Each man in the ranks was accorded a square yard of standing room, with a three-foot interval to give him free play with his weapons. Though the *triarii* retained the *hasta* for thrusting, the soldiers in the other ranks had two *pila* each. The regulation oval shield, *scutum*, was four feet long; it was replaced by the curved rectangular form at the end of the 2nd century B.C.

Usually an action commenced with skirmishing by lightly-armed troops and cavalry, after which the *hastati* moved up within range and hurled a shower of *pila*. If the lead was effective, the remainder of the legion advanced in support. The *principes* filled up the gaps between front-line maniples and the *triarii* moved out to the flanks. At close quarters, the legionary used the new type Spanish sword, the *gladius Ibericus*, another weapon adopted from enemy sources. This sword was a cut and thrust type with a long point, suitable for infantry. In the cavalry the long *spatha* was retained, with the *hasta* for a lance.

Toward the end of the 2nd century B.C., the Roman army fell under the command of a man of the people. He

[36]

was Marius of Arpinium, a former ploughboy, whose ability had gained him a staff appointment in the army of Metellus, in Numidia. During his brief career as commander—only five or six years—Marius completely changed the recruiting methods. He increased the intake of recruits by doing away with the property system. It was no longer necessary for an enlisted man to be a property owner; any penniless citizen could join the ranks.

Marius' system had far-reaching effects. By his levelling of class, he created a professional army, chiefly made up of young men who had chosen arms as their career. Though the citizen's obligation to serve was still law, it was ignored in view of the great flow of volunteers. Here were men whose life was in the army. As such, they could be drilled into evolutions far beyond the capacity of the citizen troops whose minds were in their shops and fields.

The ploughboy commander, who was elected consul six times, turned his attention to the structure of the army. He expanded the legion into 6,000 men, divided into ten units called *cohorts*. Each unit was highly trained in a form of battle drill in three ranks, so that the officers could move the cohorts on the battlefield with great precision. Through this, the legion's striking power was immensely increased.

Almost the first task for Marius was to hold back the encroaching German tribesmen in the north. He did this effectively by changing the spacing of each rank, through the use of cohorts. As these units were larger than maniples, there was a narrower gap between. Previously the headlong charge of the German tribesmen had been able to penetrate the broad gaps between the maniples. This commander did not confine his strategy to three ranks. A legion might go into action in a single rank.

The rise of Marius showed the changed structure of the Roman army as regards the officer class. During the previous century (the second before Christ), the officers were drawn only from the patrician order, the noble families, and the highest command was given to a consul. This was a great weakness, as the consul, in his office as president,

ROMAN INFANTRY, 10 B.C.

might not have seen any military service. Another difficulty was that a consul's term might expire on the eve of a battle. This was, at length, provided for by extending the consul's term as a military commander. He was then known as a proconsul.

In the people's army of the last century B.C., a staunch

[38]

body of experienced lower officers, like the centurion, provided a firm base for the whole structure. Though the Romans still lacked professional generals, promotion made possible the rise of some officers who had begun at a low level.

In the new army, training and self-confidence had produced a soldier of better quality than any before. Where previously the soldier had signed on annually for twenty campaigns, under Marius he took a single oath to bind him for the whole period of twenty years. This was the framework of a professional army, with a great raising of standards in discipline and training. It was not a state army, but one serving in loyalty to its generals.

Each legion was given a separate identity by Marius, and this was signified by an *aquila* or eagle standard. Little chapels were provided in camp for storing the eagles, which were variously adorned with wreaths, medallions, etc. The letters S P Q R seen in some pictures of standards represented the legend *Senatus Populus Que Romanos*, the senate and people of Rome. Standard-bearers, *vexillarii*, were chosen for their outstanding bravery. While on the march, they were at the head of the column, but in action they were posted with the *triarii*, to protect their precious charges.

In his drive for efficiency, Marius reorganized the soldier's personal kit, so that each man, while being self-supporting, could help to provide for communal needs. Included with the clothing in his pack, were three days' rations, a saw, a basket, an axe and a spade, a sickle, a leather thong, and an iron chain. The infantryman, *impeditus*, carried this load upon a pole over his shoulder, so that he need not unstrap a pack to remove his armour. He was nicknamed by the wits of 101 B.C. *mulus Marianus*, the mule of Marius.

Outstanding in any Roman army was the sturdy figure

of the centurion. His position was unique. In effect, he was a company sergeant major, but he held a commission. There is a hackneyed term "the backbone of the army," and this exactly fitted the centurion. It has been said that the true greatness of the Roman army lay not in its commanders but in its organization, the efficiency of the centurions, and the disciplined obedience of the common soldier.

As the name implies, the centurion was originally in charge of a hundred men, but as we have seen, the number was reduced to sixty quite early in the army's history. Under Marius, the officer in question could be promoted to senior centurion, as *primus pilus*, to be in charge of an entire cohort. He was always an experienced soldier of the ranks, outstanding for his bravery and powers of endurance. Usually he was a property owner who was not quite rich enough for the equestrian class, or a veteran recalled for service.

It was a regular practice to assign centurions to different legions at intervals, so that there was less chance of them growing familiar with the men. There seems to have been little chance of this, anyway, as one of the centurion's functions was to flog offenders with his official vine-rod, *vitis*. He was permitted to do this on his own initiative. Another unpopular aspect of his duty was to detail men of his command for guards and fatigues, though the writer Tacitus, in the 1st century A.D., hinted at bribes by which the men sometimes avoided these matters.

Undoubtedly the Roman army gained its military successes through a strict code of discipline, though, as just related, slips might occur. In the case of an actual military crime, there was sharp punishment for unit or individual. Capital crimes were desertion, mutiny, and insubordination. If a cohort was found guilty of either, regulations decreed that every tenth man should be stoned to death (*decimatio*) by soldiers of other units. Individuals who thus offended were often sentenced to beheading.

Where less serious crimes were concerned, such as a man stealing, lying, or rendering himself unfit for service, the most hated punishment was flogging by the centurion. Less severe penalties were loss of rank, or parading all day before the orderly room while clad only in a tunic, as an object of derision.

One regulation that was not strictly enforced forbade serving rankers to marry, though officers were permitted to do so. Many soldiers disregarded the ruling, and in A.D. 93 Domitian issued a decree acknowledging the marriages of veterans. These were men who had served their full terms —reduced to sixteen years by Augustus, who died A.D. 14 —and who were doing their extra four years on reserve service, without drills or fatigues.

There are many impressive features of Roman army organization that must be left out or briefly mentioned. We might glance at the duties of the *tribuni*, the staff officers of the legion, who kept the list of serving soldiers, noted casualties, dealt with applications for leave, and prepared discharge papers for time-expired men. In camp, the quartermaster, *praefectus castorum*, organized the camp and supervised artillery and missiles. He was also responsible for the camp doctor, *medici*, and the *horologiarius*, who looked after the camp water clock (a time-keeper which measured the passage of time by the dripping of known quantities of water).

Roman camps followed a set pattern. A marching camp, built at the end of a day's journey, was composed of earthworks in a rectangular form, with a surrounding ditch, and a palisade upon the earthwork. It was not intended as a fort, but simply as a guard to prevent an unhindered attack upon the tents of the unit.

Where a permanent garrison was to be maintained, the

camp's protection was reinforced with masonry. Even then, the intention was not to fight from behind the walls; Roman troops preferred to be in the open, where their training could best serve them.

A towered gateway, often with a double entrance, marked the main roadway into the fort. There were three minor gates, perhaps with towers, and turrets were placed at the rounded corners of the earthworks. Around the whole site was a double ditch, and inside the camp there was an orderly arrangement. *Principia*, the headquarters building, was sited centrally and flanked by the commandant's house and the granaries. Most of the ground space was occupied by blocks of long barracks, each building of which might house a century.

The parade ground was outside the camp, as was the bathhouse in some cases. A permanent camp like this soon collected around it a group of hutments and booths, from which local inhabitants sold wine and other attractive wares.

In the early Roman army, the majority of the recruits had provided their own arms and equipment, but in Marius' day the kit was issued. The heavy infantryman is the most familiar figure in Roman history. He wore, over the universal tunic, some form of body protection. It might be formed of leather, iron mail, metal scales, or horizontal iron bands, *lorica segmentata*. Below the cuirass, the thighs were defended by strips of guarded leather, and the curved rectangular shield could be locked with those on either side to form the well-known "tortoise," *testudo*. Under Julius Caesar (died 44 B.C.) the *pilum* was fitted with a shaft whose upper end, behind the head, was made of soft iron. This bent when striking the target, aggravating a wound, and preventing the *pilum* from being thrown back.

The legionary's cloak, of a regulation rust-red, served either as a weather garment or a blanket. When required to serve in a cold climate, the soldier was issued with leather breeches reaching well below the knee, and a woollen scarf. His footwear comprised hobnailed sandals with wooden soles, and occasionally leather buskins were worn.

In connection with issued equipment, the soldier suffered a number of stoppages from his pay, to the extent of about half the pay. According to Polybius, the Greek historian who died about 120 B.C., the legionary of his day was paid 120 *denarii* a year. It is always difficult to equate ancient coinage with changing present-day values, but the *denarius* seems to have been about 8d. or 9 cents in value. Julius almost doubled the soldier's pay, to 225 *denarii* a year, and Domitian (died A.D. 96) increased it to 300 *denarii*. A centurion of Domitian's army received 5,000 *denarii* a year, and a *primus pilus* 20,000 *denarii*.

There were other stoppages besides those for kit, as shown by a report from Domitian's forces in Egypt. One notable item was the payment for a year's food (*victum*), 240 *drachmae*. The Egyptian silver *drachma* equalled about 2d., or 2 cents, and the copper coin slightly less. A stoppage for food was apparently a regular thing. Tacitus wrote of an incident in the reign of Nero, when a plot had been discovered (Piso's conspiracy, A.D. 65) and the Emperor rewarded his guards with the free issue of food. Evidently they had paid until then.

Other items for stoppages were bedding for garrisons, subscriptions to the annual camp dinner, and *ad signa*, the soldiers' burial club! On the other hand, there was a savings bank system to encourage thrift among the men.

It is a curious point that, in spite of his hardihood, the Roman soldier was practically a vegetarian. Tacitus quoted that in one instance, at least, soldiers ate meat only when they were starving—in 69 B.C., at the siege of Tigranocerta, northern Mesopotamia. Normally the army diet was most simple—soup, bread and vegetables with lard, the drink being vinegar and water, or a little wine.

The enlisted man was kept at work in peacetime, to avoid the evils of idleness. Soldiers were employed on civil works, roads, bridges, and camp construction. They went

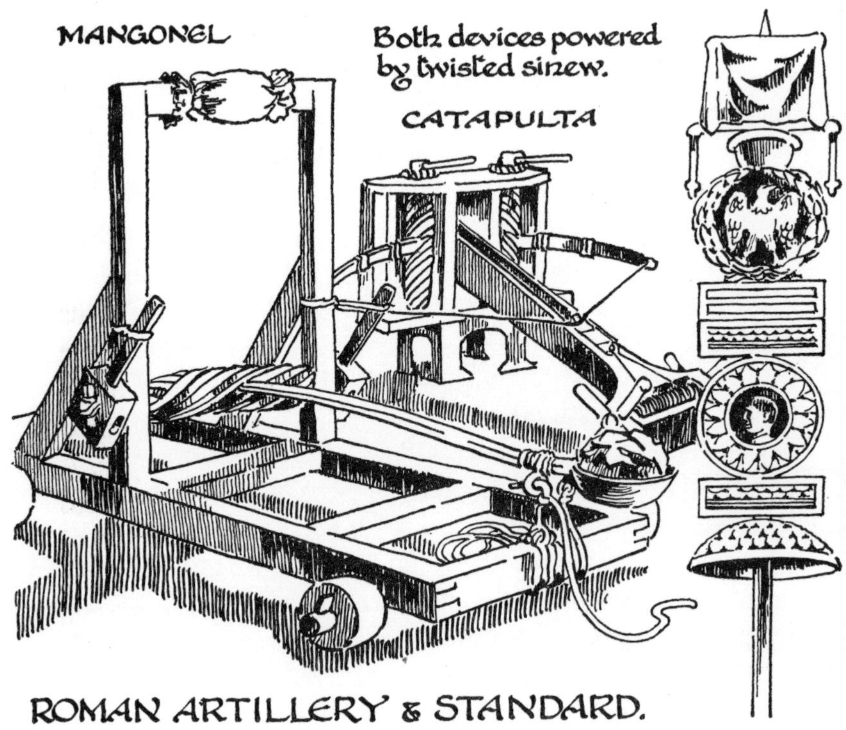

ROMAN ARTILLERY & STANDARD.

on twenty-mile marches, usually three in a month, and they carried out military exercises. While in camp, their activities closely resembled those of the 20th century soldier—guard duties at headquarters and the orderly room (*stationes*) and night guard duty (*vigiliae*). They cleaned up camp (*ad stercus*) and they cleaned weapons and armour (*armamenta*) under the armourer. Some men were

[44]

detailed to be collecting food (*cum frumentarius*) and others to be going for wine (*exit vino*).

One serious defect in the administration arose toward the end of the last century B.C. Octavius had set up a military chest (*aerarium militare*) to provide gratuities for time-expired men. He arranged a five per cent tax on inheritance, and a one per cent tax on auction sales in Rome, to raise funds for the chest. Unfortunately, this did not build enough funds, so that the men's discharge was often delayed; sometimes a legionary might serve as many as forty years before discharge. This led to mutinies in the 1st century A.D., and the whole matter remained unsettled for years.

There were a number of decorations in the army, to be awarded for notable service. One important award was the civic crown (*corona civicae*), which was available for all ranks. Tiberius (died A.D. 37) once bestowed it upon an ordinary soldier. There were various other *coronae* for officers, and bracelets, torques, and *phalerae* (medallions) for rankers and junior officers.

However, to the serving soldier there was one particular provision that ranked above awards. A legionary might be far from home, but he could still keep in touch with his family through the efficient postal service that girdled the Mediterranean. Ranging over thousands of miles, the messengers of Rome travelled the good, paved roads that made their service possible. At every twenty-five miles or so, post-houses were set up along the main roads, by the end of the last century B.C. These houses were only intended for official use. On first-class roads hostelries (*mansiones*) were built, often with veterinary surgeons living on the premises.

At a post-house the mounted messenger could exchange his tired horse for a fresh one, or, if top speed was desirable, he could pass his postbag to a fresh rider. In the same

[45]

way, relays of foot messengers using the road could rest at intermediate milehouses, and pass their letters to other runners. It was through this elaborate organization that the soldier stationed far off in Egypt or France could exchange news with those at home.

4. The Western Barbarians

When the Romans first began to spread their power outside Italy, they moved eastward and conquered Greece (197 B.C.). For more than a century, successive Roman commanders were extending and securing the eastern empire, though little progress was made toward the west. In fact, for many years western tribesmen were a menace to the safety of Rome itself.

Prominent among the savage warriors were the formidable Germanic races from beyond the western Alps. Just before Marius took command of the army, Teutons and

Cimbrians had inflicted repeated defeats upon the legions, despite organization, discipline, and skill in arms. It was understandable; barbarian tactics were entirely mass assault, a technique of swamping the opponents regardless of loss. At the end of the 2nd century B.C., Rome was

GERMAN TRIBESMEN, 100 B.C.

only saved by the skilful leadership of Marius. He crushed huge Cimbrian concentrations on either side of the Alps.

These early Germans were tall, powerful people, with long, flaxen hair and bright blue eyes. Their freeman class comprised most of the population, slaves being chiefly prisoners of war or felons. A small number of the freemen were nobles, and there was an intermediate class, *Liti*, a lower-grade freeman without the privilege of owning land.

[48]

Most freemen had their dwellings grouped in villages, and a number of villages made a "hundred." Each village had its elected chief, and a higher chief ruled each hundred; over all was the chief of the tribe. Family ties were very strong. A husband treated his wife as a respected adviser, and the children were well-disciplined. When the head of a household died, the related families were bound to guard the interests of the bereaved.

There was no distinct military body. All freemen were soldiers as a matter of course, and the men of each hundred formed a battle group of five or six thousand. At the head was the chief of the hundred.

When they were in action, the Germans employed throwing spears, *framea*, and at close quarters they wielded maces and broad axes. Their only protection was a long shield, but their attack was intimidating. They rushed upon the opponent in a frenzy, shouting and chanting, wave after wave of footmen and wild horsemen.

Marius could defeat the Germans, but he was defeated by his political enemies in the Senate, so that he retired in disgrace (100 B.C.). In that year was born Julius Caesar, who made the first Roman penetration into Germany in 58 B.C. Though Julius Caesar made no attempt at conquest, he defeated the tribes on the left bank of the Rhine in so impressive a manner that many Germans enlisted in the Roman army.

Nearly fifty years later, the Roman general, Drusus, was allotted the task of bringing Germany into subjection as a vassal state. By skilfully exploiting tribal factions, Drusus made great progress, so that after his death in 9 B.C., Tiberius was able to continue the work. Drusus had delivered a forceful opinion of the German tribesmen. He said, in effect, that the German respected nothing but strength. "He must be smitten to the dust, and struck down as he rises, and struck again as he lies groaning."

A great setback occurred in A.D. 6, when Quinctilius Varus commanded the forces in Germany. Varus was deceived by the apparent docility of the tribesmen. Having been tricked into making a long, ill-ordered march through rain and difficult country, he found his forces so hopelessly placed that he killed himself. Most of those men who did not follow suit were slaughtered as they floundered in the bogs. Only a small number escaped, and three eagles were captured.

Though Roman prestige suffered through this defeat, the balance was restored in A.D. 13 by the son of Drusus. This able commander received the name of Germanicus, both as his given name after his father and as his own well-merited title. Germanicus recovered two of the lost eagles by force of arms, and his lame brother, the emperor Claudius, later directed from Rome the finding of the third. By clever questioning of Germans in the Roman service, Claudius deduced where the third eagle was hidden, and wrote directions to his brother.

Just as Drusus himself had done, Germanicus gave to his men a solemn address upon their enemies. "The Germans," he said, "are the most insolent and boastful nation in the world when things go well with them, but in defeat they are the most cowardly and abject. . . . Stab at their faces—that is the thing most hateful to them."

Though the subjection of Germany was never completed, Roman influence among the tribesmen was profound, and a good deal of territory was gained in the south and east. While this was going on, Roman power was spreading through Gaul, which corresponded more or less to modern France. In that country there were three main divisions of people, Iberians, Belgae, and, most important, Gauls, through whom the country was then named. These were intelligent and lively people, frank and brave by nature, though when Julius Caesar entered Gaul they were living in a semi-barbaric state. Each of the clans was an entirely separate entity, with its leader, its priests, and a ruling body of warrior horsemen. A great part of the clans-people were of servile status, ministering to the fighters.

Usually the clan dwelling was a village of circular, wattled huts, but occasionally a fortress town, such as Alesia, was erected on a hilltop and surrounded with earthworks. A stronghold might be established in forest or marsh, but these places were all isolated. Through this separationist policy, the Gauls were not so difficult to over-come as the Germans, in spite of a prolonged and gallant resistance.

Some settlements had been made by Romans nearly eighty years before Julius Caesar appeared, but his was the first effort at conquest. Within eight years, by 50 B.C., the entire country was under Roman rule, and the conqueror was wise enough to see the great possibilities of civilizing the inhabitants. Julius Caesar administered the country with great tact and skill, so that, becoming completely Romanized, the Gauls reached a high degree of civiliza-tion.

It had long been established that Gallic traders from Armorica frequently took their wares into Britain across the Channel. This traffic was checked by the presence of a Roman army in Gaul, but Julius Caesar weighed the advantages of an expedition into Britain. He did not expect to colonize the country with his limited forces, but there were several reasons for making the move. An impressive stroke would raise his stock among the Roman people, with good political results. Tribute and slaves would be accept-able, and it would have an effect upon the Gauls if they saw the Britons within the Roman sphere of influence. In any case, the intending rulers of Gaul needed some know-ledge of nearby peoples.

As it happened, the plan was illjudged. Julius Caesar's

first landing, after crossing the Dover Straits, in 55 B.C., met with little success. His force, of two legions and auxiliary cavalry, was too small, so that he pushed but ten miles inland. While he was doing so, a spell of rough weather damaged his ships, so he was forced to retreat and repair them.

In the following year, Julius renewed the attack in force, with five legions. He drove across the Thames and penetrated into what is now Hertfordshire. However, it was not politic to attempt a permanent settlement, so the Roman force returned to Gaul for the second time. This apparent defeat persuaded the restless Gauls to launch simultaneous attacks upon the widely-scattered Roman camps. Their energy and bravery made them formidable, and one whole legion was wiped out.

The grand climax of the Gallic conquest was staged around the walls of Alesia, where the prince Vercingetorix was besieged. Julius Caesar was encircled in turn by a huge concentration of tribesmen, bent on raising the siege. It could not be done. The iron lines of the Romans, strewing the dead before them, beat down and scattered the unorganized attackers. With victory hot within them, the legionaries stormed over Alesia's walls. Vercingetorix, too proud to run, surrendered himself as a prisoner.

For almost a century after the death of Julius Caesar (44 B.C.) the Britons were left unmolested in their "isle of fogs." It was a kinsman, the lame, stammering Claudius, who followed the great commander's lead in A.D. 43. Claudius was Emperor of the Romans, though he was no soldier. His extensive studies had shown him how the British organized their forces, and when he planned the invasion of Britain his preparations included some unusual items.

Most prominent among the British warriors was the charioteer. Though this was an outdated system, it was still effective. Unlike other war vehicles, the British chariot was open in front, with two spirited horses harnessed to a broad, flat pole. A noble drove and commanded the chariot, and two fighters rode with him. Sometimes one of the fighters would run out along the pole to fling javelins from between the horses' heads.

These chariots were capable of quite high speed, and the skilled driver could veer off at a tangent while moving fast. In action, the tactics were to race the chariots in a column straight at the opposing foot soldiers. If their line broke before the menace, a shower of short javelins fell among the scattered men. Where the opponents showed no sign of giving way, the chariots would wheel off along the front, with the fighters flinging their javelins as they passed. It might be possible to circle the enemy formation, throwing in another volley of spears at the rear. After several forays of this kind, the fighters dismounted to go in with the infantry.

In spite of the common idea that knives were attached to the chariot wheels, there is no written evidence to prove this, and no remains of the kind have ever been found.

Claudius held the opinion that, man for man, the British foot soldier was at least equal to the Roman, but that the Briton's arms and his method of fighting were more suited to single combat. The British broadsword was an unhandy weapon at close quarters, and the leather buckler was too small to give cover against the *pila*. These circumstances assured Claudius that with a sufficient force he could over-comé the infantry, so he concentrated on meeting the chariot attack.

Early in August, A.D. 43, the Emperor sent out an expedition to Britain, under the command of Aulus Plautius, who was instructed to transmit a beacon signal when his losses reached 2,000 killed and wounded. On receiving the signal, Claudius sailed with a fleet of triremes, and by the beginning of September the Emperor had joined forces with Aulus before a stockaded British stronghold near Romford, in Essex.

Claudius now assembled his weapons of psychological warfare, to play upon the superstitious nature of the Britons. The latter believed that a gigantic bird, the Heron King, haunted the nearby marshes in times of peril, so a Gaulish soldier on stilts, fearfully disguised, startled the outposts in the misty dawn.

When the first column of British chariots rattled down upon the dim masses of the enemy, the horses balked at the edge of the banks of mist. A weird, foul smell pervaded the mist. It came from a line of camels, creatures completely unknown to the Britons, As the leading chariots hovered in confusion, a detachment of legionaries showered them with *pila*.

Meanwhile, Caractacus, the famous British leader, led an attack on the Roman flank, with 3,000 chariots in his wake. Just as the racing warriors were coming within range, there was an outburst of frightful noise and fire. The oncoming chariots were in a rain of blazing balls of pitch. Dozens of them collided, the charioteers dragging along the ground with the reins around their waists. Into the chaos sped a storm of lead bolts from the crowd of Balearic slingers who suddenly appeared from the mist.

As a disordered mass of chariotry swerved aside from the wreckage and tore on, the leading vehicles suddenly piled up on one another. In a mad confusion of squealing horses, splintering wood, and frantic yells, a great heap of ruin reared above the foot-high tripropes that Claudius had caused to be arranged in the grass. While men and horses threshed in the tangle, around them thundered a wild noise of drums, and black devils appeared, to thrust with long spears at the helpless warriors.

This was the most extraordinary victory of ancient

times. Claudius' negroes were the finishing touch to a welter of superstitious terror for the hapless Britons. That day marked the beginning of the Roman occupation. Though for some time ferocious uprisings recurred, Britain was to be a Roman colony for nearly 400 years.

5. The New Master Race

True to their system of organization, the Roman occupation army laid out a pattern of fortified camps throughout England. They did not penetrate far into the wild mountains of Wales, or into Scotland, but their main fort sites are marked today by place names ending in "chester" or "caster," from *castra*, camp.

Early in the 2nd century A.D. the most famous Roman defensive work in Britain was constructed. Hadrian, who ruled the empire from A.D. 117 to A.D. 138, visited Britain in A.D. 122, and set going the great project known as

Hadrian's Wall. It stretched for seventy-three miles, from the Tyne to the Solway Estuary, with an average height of twenty feet. Clay and sods were used for part of the western end, though this was later built up in stone and concrete like the rest. In general, the wall was about ten feet thick, with forts at intervals—sixteen forts altogether, with intermediate towers at every mile. Forts and mile castles covered steps up to the walk on top of the wall and the gateways through it.

Manpower for the tremendous task was furnished by the army, with some recruited help from the local men. Each section of the wall was allotted to a century, and the builders placed a simple "trade mark" on the finished length. When completed, the wall was intended as a deterrent, not an impregnable work. It hindered the incursions of the wild Northern clansmen, and prevented them from driving home cattle stolen in a raid. For this reason, the legions had little to do with the actual manning of the wall; the garrison of the forts comprised nearly 10,000 auxiliaries, one cohort per fort, with connecting patrols in the mile castles. A short distance behind the wall was a chain of large legionary camps, each connected with the forts by roads. In the event of an attack, the auxiliaries held on while the legions came up.

An interesting feature of Roman Britain was this question of auxiliaries. In all other conquered lands, the army had taken in natives to train. This was not done in Britain. It seemed as if the Roman authorities feared to add to the fighting qualities of the Briton by giving him Roman training.

Through the increasing intake of non-Romans, the army was changing its character. In the reign of Hadrian —who was a Spaniard—there were about 220,000 soldiers all told, but the majority were recruited from the provinces. A foreign soldier who enlisted was accorded citizenship, so the fiction of a Roman citizen's army was maintained. As the army's commitments were so great, extending thousands of miles throughout the Mediterranean, the citizens of Rome rarely saw the march of the legions as in former days.

Rome itself was declining. It was becoming difficult for the government to find enough money, and army pay fell into arrears during the reign of Marcus Aurelius (died 180). In lieu of money, the Emperor had to pay some troops with grain, and frontier units were allotted land instead of pay. This land was useless to the men unless they settled on it, so many soldiers married and lived in huts on their frontier posts. They were only called upon to serve in the event of a raid, so they degenerated into undisciplined militia, called *limitanei*, frontiersmen.

These were the seeds of destruction, and two circumstances nourished the seeds. In their eagerness to impose their way of life upon subject nations, the Romans did not consider that civilization fostered independent thought. Accordingly, many provincial peoples felt themselves the equal of their masters. The other grave feature was a deficiency in the Roman constitution—there was no legal and established method of choosing a new Emperor, to maintain uninterrupted the supreme authority of Rome.

Under these conditions, the army was destined to gain civil power. A true Roman citizen was scarcely to be found in the ranks, and for that reason the old Roman discipline and army structure declined. An army composed of provincials soon relapsed into the barbarian massed formation, so Roman military power died.

This was not all. After the death of Marcus Aurelius, a number of soldiers' factions struggled among themselves to enthrone Emperors from their own ranks. Power was eventually seized by a rough and energetic soldier named Septimius Severus, who raised to high civil and military posts his comrades of low birth. In this way, the whole government system was debased, and when the soldier-Emperor's line died out in 235, chaos followed. In a number of the provinces, the ill-disciplined troops there set up rival candidates for the throne of the Mediterranean world. Time after time election was followed by assassination, so that during a period of ninety years, the Romans were ruled in turn by eighty emperors, all soldiers.

For some time—centuries, in fact—the German tribes had been freely admitted among Romans. Their nobles had intermarried, and the degenerate Roman army of the 4th century was largely composed of old-type German fighting groups, with their mass tactics. By a curious turn of fate, this Germano-Roman army was defeated in 378 by another German tribe, the Visigoths or West Goths. These roving barbarians infiltrated to the south and west, from their own lands east of the Danube. Steadily increasing pressure and reckless savagery in attack brought them to the very gates of Rome. The year 410 saw the Visigoths triumphing in the streets of the fallen city, theirs to burn and plunder.

In its days of glory, the Roman empire had been greater than any that had gone before it. It fell like a Colossus, ruins scattered far and wide. A mere dream, then, those tramping legions, the hard-bitten soldiers of long before, steeped in victory, a deadly, efficient fighting machine. No more the life of the queenly, gracious city, thronged with the rich and noble, bejewelled with borrowed art, and ruling the ends of the civilized world.

The outermost ripple of that wave of calamity reached the shores of the Isle of Fogs, and brought away the garrisons there—only the garrisons. There was no room on the crowded transports for civilians and their dependents. Only young, able Britons were crammed aboard with the troops, and as the deep-laden vessels drew away from the shore, they left wild terror behind. An enemy was at the gates—a savage, seafaring enemy, whose attacks upon the eastern shore had been repelled by Roman power until that grievous day.

BRITISH CHIEF, c. 570.

From Germany they came, akin to the conquerors whose fighting men then revelled in the streets of Rome. These seaborne invaders were Saxon men of the north, brawny, tall, and flaxen-haired like those of other tribes.

The Saxons were truly German in their regard for kinship and clan grouping, and they were exceptional in devo-

[60]

tion to peaceful arts. There was much kindness and good nature in their dealings with their own kin, and they were enthusiastic farmers. Yet those of their number who sailed with their chosen leaders on raiding forays displayed the fiercest brutality, courage, and loyalty.

These men were chiefly deep-sea fishermen and seal hunters; they were equally at home in battle with a wild sea or a ferocious enemy. That is not to say that the other Saxons, who followed the plough, were in anyway milk sops. They would bear up in the fight as staunchly as their brothers, when called upon.

During the winter months, when the undecked boats could not put to sea, the chieftain made merry in his barn-like log hall with the freemen of his marauding group. Seated around the "ale board," the revellers ate hugely, and swilled their muddy ale. Their entertainment was nothing but their own bellowing of drinking songs, unless some minstrel came among them to divert them with a hero ballad.

At length, when spring made it possible to put to sea, the chieftain prepared to lead his predatory wolves along the coast to devour their victims. These men could not be classed as soldiers, for there was no question of regular pay, merely shared plunder. This could be said of all the barbarian races whose heel was planted on the civilized world after the Roman collapse. Several centuries were to pass before the soldier receiving pay appeared again. However, the savage warriors formed a link between the Roman empire and the Middle Ages, so they have their place.

Robber Saxons of the type who first landed in Britain were organized in a manner unlike the German tradition. In the raiders' ranks, the main factor was not kinship but the discipline of a ship's crew, and allegiance to the leader of the fleet.

When the ships were ready, the chief presented to each

captain the prized gift, a sword. Each follower received a pair of iron-headed spears, with seven-foot shafts of ash, and a circular, wooden shield bound with iron. The men fought in their woollen tunics, but the leaders wore costly shirts of mail.

Those first expeditions into helpless England were purely for the sake of plunder. There is no written record of the horrors that the Britons endured during that span of two centuries that we call the Dark Ages. Long after the first brutal devastation, about 540, the historian Gildas wrote from hearsay:

"Every colony is levelled to the ground by the stroke of the battering ram. The inhabitants are slaughtered along with the guardians of their churches, priests and people alike, while the sword gleamed on every side, and the flames crackled around. How horrible to behold in the midst of the street the tops of towers torn from their lofty hinges, the stones of high walls, holy altars, mutilated corpses. ... Of the miserable remnant, some flee to the hills, only to be captured and slain in heaps: some, constrained by famine, come in and surrender themselves to be slaves forever to the enemy. ... Others wailing bitterly pass overseas."

Close behind the brutal thrust of the pirates came the settlers with their farming implements, seeking a land that afforded more encouraging soil than the sands and marshes of Northern Germany.

It seems likely that, when the wave of destruction first flowed over the country, the invaders were working under a single command, as a *host*. Before that wave, the great Roman houses sank in ruins, and strong Roman camps and earthworks were beaten flat by a people with no military science. When the occupation began, the invaders fell into their original groups, as on shipboard.

The settlements, spread over the southern half of England, continued the seagoing division of the people into shiploads. Each group of villages, irrespective of clan, became the holding of the *thegn* (pronounced *thane*) who had commanded the fleet concerned. With their hands between his, the menfolk swore to serve, with theirs sons, in peace and war. They should work the thegn's land, as well as the land they held under him, arfd all men should be at his call for war. In this way, pirate and farmer became bound to the land.

The better to maintain a fighting force, it was the law that all fit males between sixteen and sixty should be liable to train in arms as the *fyrd*. They were bound to serve on call for a period not exceeding two months. A mass of men gathered like this would be armed only with spear and shield; swords and mail coats were still exclusive to the leaders.

Here we see a semi-civilized community whose men were territorial soldiers at need, but whose chief inclination was toward agriculture. Though there was a great deal of rivalry and petty war betwen the great chiefs or kings, the country settled into a relatively peaceful farming life, so that Christianity revived, and spread widely through the land. However, at the end of the 8th century, a storm began to move in from the northeast.

Scandinavian peoples are of the same racial origin as the Germans, from what is known as Nordic (northern) stock. There are the same characteristics—tall stature, blond hair, and blue eyes, and the adventurous spirit. It was a small band of Norwegian rovers, in three longships, who first made contact with the British shores, in Wessex. This was the ancient name ("West Saxons") of the extreme southern part of England, reaching from Devon almost to London.

The Scandinavian newcomers were called *Vikings*, meaning warriors. They differed from the Saxons in that they loved fighting for its own sake, with trade as a secondary consideration. Their menfolk fell into three main divisions—*eorls* (from which arose the rank of *earl*), *carls*, and *thralls*; in effect, nobles, freemen, and bondsmen. It is true that the families of the eorls were extensive, through

NORSEMEN, c. 800.

the practice of polygamy and the small heed that was paid to illegitimacy. For this reason there were, among the leaders of the nation, numbers of restless young men, of high birth and spirits, and eager for adventure.

Among the Vikings there was an extraordinary degree of personal vanity. The young warrior was proud of his sword, his helmet and mail shirt, his scarlet cloak, and his long fair hair. No man was a man until he had ventured

[64]

out to blood his sword on a piratical voyage. In fact, a young, fit man who stayed at home was derided even by the girls, who were tall and strong like the Spartan girls of the classical age. It was not unknown for a girl to arm at all points, like a man, and take a man's place on a raiding longship.

When shiploads of these formidable people stormed ashore, the Saxons were at a grave disadvantage. Apart from the fact that the habit of war was not so strong, they had never been organized like the newcomers. With dismay, the defenders saw longships penetrating far into the waterways of the east, where the raiders seized horses from the East Anglian pastures. They used the horses simply as rapid transport, and left them when falling upon the settlements to kill and destroy. Every invader was fully armed—sword, helmet, and mail shirt—and the Vikings made use of the bow, which for superstitious reasons was no part of the Anglo-Saxon's war gear.

It was ironical that the Saxon's conversion to Christianity was the indirect cause of invasion. The richness of the church vessels and ornaments formed the chief lure for the rapacious Vikings, with women and slaves as a sideline. Though the defenders fought back gallantly, they were outclassed. They had forgotten the ferocity of their pirate ancestors, and their arms were of the old-time casting and thrusting type.

Norwegians and Danes, wave after wave, harried the southern half of England. Toward the end of the 9th century their fleets often numbered 300 ships, each with a hundred men aboard. The legendary Alfred of Wessex (died 901) raised a fleet of warships to meet the invaders at sea, and (contrary to Saxon ideas), he mounted some of his forces on horseback to attack overland.

By this means both sides disposed of horsemen, but not as cavalry; the military mind had progressed no further

[65]

than mounted infantry, riding to the fight. Alfred was forced to maintain his thegns and their freemen on a permanent war footing. This made the men more or less professional soldiers.

After many years of bloodshed, after the establishment of a Danish community in northern England, Danes and Saxons commingled under a Danish king. Canute, son of Sweyn Forkbeard the Viking, reigned from 1016 to 1036, and he made a further step towards the professional army. He established a permanent royal guard of *huscarls* (house carls), picked men of good physique and proved skill in arms. These household troops were equipped with the best that the age could provide—well wrought Continental mail shirts, and fine swords.

Originally the men were all Scandinavians, but Saxons were admitted soon after the guard's formation. Service in the unit was strictly on payment—the men owed no dues as landholders. They were professional soldiers drawing the King's pay, though the actual amount was not clear.

While the Vikings were hurrying their longships in search of plunder, they did not confine themselves to Britain. Viking adventurers traversed the Mediterranean, and reached overland to the Black Sea. Their venture into Britain ran parallel with another foray just as important.

In A.D. 911, Vikings under Rolfe the Ganger established a bridgehead in northwestern France carved from the territory of the once warlike Franks. The latter were of German origin, and though they were now Christians, their forefathers had been as ferocious as any of that race. Axe-carrying men, like so many German tribes, the Franks had taken their name from the weapon (*francisca*). It was wielded in the hand, or thrown accurately for some distance.

Sidonius Apollinaris (430–88) described the Franks as "monsters.... From the top of their red skulls descends their hair, knotted on the front, and shaved in the nape of the neck." The tribesmen of the 5th century had long moustaches, and they wore tight knee-length tunics with short sleeves. Their wide girdles were studded with metal, and a baldric or swordbelt suspended the sword on the left side.

During the reign of the Charlemagne (*Carolus Magnus*, Charles the Great), 771–814, the loosely-allied clans of the Franks were linked in closer unity. The Frankish warriors learned the use of the stirrup, which had been brought west by the ruthless Huns from Asia in the early 5th century. While Norsemen in England were using the horse merely as rapid transport, the Frank was riding into action with a spear couched beneath his arm. Men had ridden

[67]

with the spear in the armies of the early empires, but without the advantage of the feet braced in stirrups to deliver the spear-point.

Barely a century had passed since the illustrious reign of Charlemagne, when the Norsemen under Rolfe the Ganger settled in France. Yet in that space the empire and influence of the able ruler had fallen to ruin, and the country was helpless. Rolfe was baptized. His men dutifully obeyed his command, and followed their leader's example.

Rolfe married Gisela, daughter of the Frankish king Charles the Simple, and received as her wedding portion the land that he had already won with the sword. Norsemen thus became Frenchmen, but they called their country Northmandy, the land of the Northmen. Later the name was corrupted to Normandy.

In that foreign land, far removed from their native shores, the Vikings built up a relic of ancient times—the military state. Though the service was not full-time, as in a standing army, it took precedence over everything else in time of war. The call-up was based on the holding of land.

Among the Normans, men were divided into four main classes, with the ruler, entitled the Duke, as head of State. Landholdings were allotted by the Duke, with large areas for the premier noblemen, the barons, who literally divided the country between them. These grants of leased land were made on condition that the barons served the king in war, together with their subordinates.

Each baron divided his territory among his following of knights. A holding in this subdivision might comprise a town and several villages, with their surrounding lands. In return, the knight swore to serve the lord in war, as well as paying dues for his holding. The people living upon the knight's *manor* rented their pieces of land on terms of

[68]

service to the knight in war, work on the knight's own land, and payment in crops. This was the *feudal* system, from the Scandinavian *feu*, a permanent landholding. Sometimes the word was rendered as *fee*, as for a knight's fee or land grant.

NORMANS, 11TH CENTURY.

When the Norman forces were in action, they were divided into three main groups—archers as the long-range striking unit, cavalry for shock action, and footmen with spears as support. Only the cavalry were protected to any extent, in pointed helmets with *nasals* (noseguards), and mail shirts (*hauberks*). The most outstanding soldier of their race was born in 1027—William, son of Duke Robert "the Devil." Having succeeded to the Dukedom when he

[69]

was only eight, William became a redoubtable soldier while still a boy.

In 1066, when a Norman invasion force of 12,000 soldiers landed in southern England near Hastings, William was at their head. His strategy brought about the defeat of the first English standing army. In this way England fell once more under the heel of a foreign invader.

The Norman army had been assembled largely on a voluntary basis, as the law only permitted the overlord to call a man for forty days' military service at a time. Still, with the prospect of loot in a conquered country the men freely waived that clause. Their leader's reputation assured them of a profitable venture.

William's immense personal strength and skill in arms literally carried the army along. When the shock tactics of his cavalry were neutralized by the steep slope of Senlac Hill, where the Saxon huscarles surrounded their king, the Duke played another card. A powerful body of archers formed part of his forces, and these were organized to shoot a dropping shower of arrows upon the stubborn defenders. When at last the bowmen were recalled, few were left alive upon the hilltop. King, earls, and all were mingled in a soldier's death.

6. Soldiers in the Crusades

A striking effect of the conquest was England's closer alliance with the Continent. For many years the subjected country was ruled in conjunction with Normandy, and a further link was forged in 1096. At that date individual soldiers from England and national forces from France, Germany and Italy, were combined in an expeditionary force bound for Palestine. Jerusalem, long held by tolerant Arabs, had fallen into the hands of Turks. These had enslaved or killed numbers of Christian pilgrims journeying to the Holy City. Christianity was sufficiently new in

Western Europe to arouse militant zeal, so the First Crusade was set in train to recapture Jerusalem.

This was the first western example of a military union of nations to fight in such a cause, and at such a distance. In the combined army, foot soldiers were of small importance, mere camp guards and workmen, for the mounted knight was the basis of the offensive force. Equipment and horses were much the same as those of thirty years before—hauberk, pointed helmet with vertical nasal, and kite shield, long-pointed to guard the rider's leg. A heavy-limbed horse, like a cart horse, bore the knight into action with his lance and sword.

Though enthusiasm was a valuable asset to the soldiers of the First Crusade, there were endless practical difficulties of organization. Apparently the nobles and their following travelled independently to Constantinople, the assembly point, but what an enormous undertaking it must have been! In all, thousands of men and horses, with war gear, baggage, provisions, and fodder were transported for distances up to 2,000 miles by clumsy wagon or tiny, open ship. If we consider what a vast quantity of food only 1,000 men needed in a week, it shows something of the supply difficulty. Problems of overwhelming quantities abounded—only four pints of water per head for 1,000 men every day demanded hundreds of gallons. The sanitation problem, the ordure of 1,000 men and hundreds of horses to be disposed of—such recurrent matters had to be handled somehow, in the hit-or-miss manner of the time.

Scarcely any of the leaders or the men had any experience of the subtropical climate. They knew nothing of the enemy's tactics, his arms, or the forces that he disposed. Very soon it appeared as if everything was leagued against them. A scorching sun heated the iron mail to an unbearable degree, so that a loose surcoat had to be worn over it—another problem of supply. The precious horses had to be coddled and protected against the ills of the climate and the maddening flies. Water for man and horse was more precious than the fabled gold mines of the East, and food supplies were menaced by heat, dust, and flies.

MEDIÆVAL
CROSSBOWMAN,

On their march southeast from Constantinople to cross Asia Minor, the western soldiers met their enemy for the first time. It was at Dorylaeum; hardly a fifth of their journey had been covered. As it happened, the army had

[73]

divided into two parallel columns marching at several miles' distance.

Upon the eastward column came a cloud of lightly-equipped Turks, unarmoured, and riding small, fast horses. As they rode around the confused mass of Christians, the attackers poured in showers of arrows from their short, strong bows. There was no formation at which the knights could charge; their nimble enemy was three times as fast as they, and the irreplaceable warhorses went down one after another.

The Westerners were in poor case. Had not their comrades of the other column come up in time, there would have been a dire slaughter. Turkish strategy was at fault in this; the archers were so engrossed in their sport that they neglected a prime military precaution—the guard at the rear. Amid the triumphant yells of the surrounded Christians, the newcomers brought down their points and charged home. Caught between two fires, the Muslims were completely routed.

Such a defeat discouraged the Turks from further pitched battles in Asia Minor, but conditions and the harassing by Turkish mounted archers played havoc with the marching force. The countryside had been wasted by Turkish action, so that the western army could not "live on the country," in the haphazard mediaeval style. Those knights who had lost their horses found it intolerable to march in their dragging mail shirts, which weighed so wearily upon their shoulders.

At length, the battered and much-thinned army reached the vicinity of Jerusalem, and positive action was taken in a siege. Here the attackers put to use the stout timbers so painfully dragged to the scene, in order to make assault towers. These were higher than the city walls—great unwieldy things, lurching madly as they were pushed and towed forward on their solid wooden wheels. Their progress was marked by the slaughter of unprotected foot soldiers, as these sweated to bring the monsters close to the city wall. Fire arrows, rocks, and balls of blazing material rained upon the towers, but they were guarded from fire by wetted horsehides, carefully kept against this day.

Above each tower-top projected a long drawbridge, standing vertically. It concealed the opening of a small cabin, served by a rear ladder, and in this cabin the assault party waited.

As the rocking of the tower ceases, the hidden attackers brace themselves for furious action. The drawbridge drops with a crash upon the crenellated wall. Daylight floods into the dark cabin, with the hysterical screeching of the Turks. Head down—shield up before the face, a hurtling rush across the iron-banded timbers, arrows and stones rattling around. A despairing yell as a comrade goes over the edge, the rest bundling anyhow off the end of the drawbridge on to the crowded wallwalk. Huddled together as they are, the Turks defeat themselves. The solid mass of mailed soldiers strikes them like a rock, smashing a foothold among them. Hew and heave for a frantic minute, steel and iron clinking together, and the bridgehead is won.

At several points around the circuit, the same kind of struggle was going on. Tearing up the tower ladders and through those hard-won entrances, the following troops poured in.

Jerusalem was taken, but the sequel was ghastly. In storming a city, it was always difficult to restrain the poorly-disciplined troops when the defence collapsed. Through the streets of Jerusalem streamed the soldiers of a Christian army, followers of the doctrine of mercy and brotherhood. Like insane butchers, they destroyed every man, woman, and child before them. Deaf and blind to anything like pity, no screams or prayerful hands could arrest the slaughterers, and the gutters ran with blood before the tardy leaders could regain control.

This was a feature to be expected. A mediaeval army was greatly inferior to the armies of antiquity as regards structure, organization, and training. It tended to degenerate into an uncontrollable rabble in adversity, or when inflamed by victory. There was none of the ingrained discipline of the Roman legionary in the ranker serving with a crusading army.

Another factor that told very heavily was the variety of motive which impelled soldiers to take part in the Crusades. Their consent was needed, as the feudal obligation only covered a forty-day campaign. Perhaps thirty per cent were urged by religious enthusiasm; another forty per cent indulged an adventurous and roving spirit, while the remainder were in frankly for what they could gain. Even today, whenever a great upheaval takes place in a community, many of its supporters are seeking only their own advantage. Our mediaeval soldier had little to lose in the way of home comfort.

During the 12th century the chief heads of state in Europe were making the effort to build up reliable fighting forces. In England, some significant moves were made by successive monarchs of that century. For instance, Henry I (1100–1135) paid attention to the skilled archery of the Welsh. Perhaps he recalled tales of the Norman arrow hail. Throughout England, the cult of the bow was fostered, and peasants were encouraged in it. Sunday being a workless day, the butts were set up (large barrels of earth to back up the targets). By the King's decree, a man was absolved of crime should he accidentally kill another while shooting at the butts.

This was the means to allow the foot-soldier to win his place in the fighting ranks. Success was not immediate, though the King made great use of his archers against cavalry at Beaumont, in 1125. A missile force that could cut up the all-powerful horsemen before they were within lance length—that was the goal.

As if to counter the infantry move, a French training method was brought to England during King Henry's reign—the staged horseback combat known as the tournament. Of all the war sports this was the most spectacular, with mounted knights dashing against each other, lance in rest. At that time the use of the lance was vastly different from that of later days. In attacking an armoured opponent, full force and a follow-through were employed, to hurl the other from the saddle. Centuries later, when the use of armour had died out, the horseman tried to engage his lance lightly, so that he could free it after a short penetration.

All early mediaeval training was simply the handling of arms. No attempt was made to exercise the soldiers in concerted movement, or to train the leaders in control and direction. This was the greatest single fault in military practice of the 12th century—there was no cohesion, each army being a chance alliance of unrelated units. No co-operative arrangements existed for food supplies or medical care, and there was no suggestion of quarters. Service in such an army meant an eternal struggle for food while on the march, horsemeat after a battle, and probably a bed on the bare ground. Often a commander was forced to retreat simply because the country around was bare of food, and a powerful enemy prevented an advance.

King Henry II of England (1154–1189) permitted men to buy themselves out of their service obligations, and with part of the money he hired mercenary troops, that is, soldiers owing no allegiance, who served simply for money. This provided the nucleus of an army at need, and as reinforcement he invoked the feudal law, which obliged every three knights to equip one of their number for active service. In 1181, the King revived the old Assize of Arms, to form a national militia, like the fyrd. These were the decrees:

1. Every holder of one knight's fee shall have a coat of mail, helmet, shield, and lance; every knight as many such equipments as there are fees in his domain.
2. Every free layman possessing sixteen marks in chattels (belongings) or rent shall keep one such equipment (one mark = 13s. 4d. then).
3. Every free layman having ten marks as above to keep *haubergeon* (short sleeveless mail coat), chaplet (cap) of iron, and lance.
4. All burgesses and freemen to keep a *wambais* (padded leather body defense), iron chaplet, and lance.

Arrangements of this kind were only provisions for an emergency force. As yet there was no standing army in England, and no royal bodyguard such as the pre-Conquest kings had possessed. The only professional soldiers that Henry II could command were his hired Brabant troops from Flanders. These were unreliable material. Men whose livelihood depended on keeping a whole skin did not take undue risks in battle.

One of the greatest difficulties in ruling 12th-century England was the existence of private armies. These were the personal retainers of barons and knights under the feudal system, servants and landworkers partly trained in arms. There was always a strong temptation to employ an armed force in personal quarrels, or even in rebellion against the King. A royal provision against the last-named action was the issue of licences for castle-building. Henry II was particularly notable for his ruthless destruction of "adulterine" or unlicensed castles.

Military arrangements in Europe resembled those in

England. A form of feudal service obtained in France, with the same effect when a muster was called. The vanguard comprised those who had some experience of war, and the remainder was simply an armed mob. When the crossbow became widely known, early in the 12th century, it was a popular Continental field weapon. Though it was more suitable for use behind defensive works, the crossbow was equal to the longbow in range, and the wounds made by its thick quarrels were severe.

In a French army preparing for action, discipline and control were noticeably lacking. The foot soldiers could not withstand a charge by cavalry, so the first stage of an action was always the disorderly flight of the infantry. They remained in confusion until their own cavalry attacked, when they followed up to hamstring the enemy horses and kill the wounded. As regards their leaders, the French chronicler Brenneville recorded: "Few [lords] were slain, for they were covered in iron, and strove rather to take one another that they might hold each other to ransom rather than to kill one another."

This ransom-seeking outlook resolved the engagement into a number of battling cavalry groups. Such an ill-organized offensive made it almost impossible to regroup forces for a collective blow, or to restore morale after a setback. This was a feature of several Anglo-French battles of the Middle Ages.

Germany as a nation did not exist during that period, but its various states were subjected to the feudal overlordship of dukes and princelings, between whom there was recurrent strife. No army at that stage could be a really effective fighting unit, due to the great cleavage between the mounted man and the foot soldier. On the one hand there was lofty contempt, as for a peasant rabble, and on the other hand glowering resentment.

Undoubtedly the true military organizations of the

Middle Ages were the great religious orders, the Knights Templar and the Hospitallers.

Originally, the Templars were a volunteer group of knights who had vowed to give protection to pilgrims on the roads leading to Jerusalem. In 1118, the group became established in headquarters near the Temple in Jerusalem, and the organization—international in character—became the symbol of militant Christianity. The knights took vows like monks. Individuals owned no property (though the Order became wealthy) and they were pledged to obedience and a celibate life. These were soldiers of an entirely new type, a living spearhead for Christians against Moslems. Their symbol was a red cross upon a white ground. This has given the idea that all crusading troops wore the same insignia, but in fact they varied according to the country; the English cross was white at first.

When the Templars were well established, a similar body appeared as the Knights Hospitaller. These soldiers of the Church belonged to an Order that was a century older than the Templars. A hospital for pilgrims had been established by churchmen in Jerusalem, but for many years it was purely a religious centre. When it became a militant unit, the Hospitallers wore white crosses upon red as a distinguishing mark.

Throughout the 12th century, the influence of the twin orders spread rapidly. Though their region of operations remained in the East, control and organization was established in many European countries. Recruits flowed in at houses provided for that purpose, where knights whose active service was over could live in retirement. These places were still classed as religious houses, but the soldier chief of each house was styled "Commander."

At a time when army organization was extremely sketchy, the Orders set a fine example. Their forces comprised infantry as well as knights; foot soldiers were termed *servientes*, or serving members—later corrupted to *sergeant*. Occasionally, the knights fielded light mounted archer skirmishers on the Turkish plan.

Long after the Crusades had ended (in the mid-13th century), the militant Church continued the defence of the Mediterranean against the Turk. It is true that the Templars were suppressed in 1312, but the Hospitallers' final home in Malta gave them a new title, the Knights of St. John. Though its career as a military movement ended in the early 19th century, the Order's Maltese cross and its name are still maintained in the great public service organization, the St. John Ambulance Brigade.

Having surveyed the finest mediaeval military groups, we should now discuss the greatest early mediaeval soldier. Richard Plantagenet, Richard I of England, Richard Cœur de Lion, has been the subject of many romantic stories. He was king for only ten years (1189–99), and a thoroughly ineffectual king at that, but he was a soldier. In the Third Crusade (1190), Richard showed that warfare to him was a science as well as a pleasure. His ideas on military strategy made him stand out among the bumbling want-wits of his time. No other commander had shown himself so resourceful in the face of an unpredictable enemy. Though he new nothing of Moslem warfare at the outset, he set himself to learn it, and to devise suitable tactics.

Richard's noble and skilful opponent was Saladin (died 1193). The English king guarded against the latter's encircling tactics by marching along the Palestine coast before turning inland to Jerusalem. He employed the two militant Orders to guard his front and rear, and he maintained close order on the march. Even at the pitched battle of Arsouf, his admirable discipline kept his forces steady and unbroken under the Moslem archery for several hours.

Richard's strategy was to encourage the Turkish forces

to close in during their attacks, until they should be so closely engaged that he could charge with effect. At Arsouf the plan worked almost to perfection, and still the English commander's discipline held good. He was able to restrain the charge from becoming a wild scramble; the troops were re-formed for a fresh concerted blow after each stage of the advance, and pursuit was finally called off while still under control. It was an admirable display of ability in command, far in advance of Richard's time.

7. Service in the Middle Ages

Progress in mediaeval troop-training was slow. The mob system was still prevalent at the beginning of the 14th century, and the English army was as poor as any in that respect. Yet during the new century the English leaped ahead of all Continental armies by developing the long-range striking force in a manner never seen before. This was partly due to the re-enactment of the Assize of Arms by both Henry III (1216–72) and Edward I (1272–1307). According to Edward's decree in 1285, a first-class freeman had to maintain a horse, a hauberk of iron, a sword,

and a knife. Second- and third-class freemen were combined to form four groups, two of which were obliged to
keep bows.

Those early Welsh bowmen of Henry I had laid the
foundation of the best missile force of the Middle Ages.
Regular training at the butts, and the developed skill of
bowyers and fletchers (arrow makers) had made English
archery supreme. The best bows were formed with the
spokeshave from a piece of yew wood, and there was an
art in producing the required degree of taper from the
middle to the ends. A year could be occupied in treating
the wood and arranging suitable seasoning, but the bow
was then fit to serve for scores of years.

When not in use, the bow was kept unstrung, to maintain the spring by allowing it to relax; the string itself
was made of twisted gut or sinew. Authorities differ as to
the length of the arrow, and some do not accept that the
clothyard or ell (forty-five inches) was the true figure.
This does not seem out of the question with a six-foot bow.

When called for active service, the English archer was
almost unprotected, for his activities needed free movement. His head was guarded by an iron cap, and occasionally a man had a collar of mail upon his shoulders, but
otherwise he wanted nothing except his ordinary clothes.
A pouch at his belt held his bowstring, with other small
necessities, and a stout knife was thrust through between
the pouch straps. Upon his left forearm was a leather
bracer to take the rub of the string, and a stall was worn
on the first two fingers of the right hand.

It is a remarkable thing that, at a time when army
organization was most haphazard, there should have
emerged such a powerful factor. After some success against
the Scots, English archers excelled themselves in action
with the French at Crécy in 1346. The tall, long-limbed
archers were fielded in the forefront of the English forces,

disposed in fairly open order. Each man had a quiver with twenty-four arrows, and provision was made to keep up the supply for a reasonable time, from wagons at the rear. It was customary for a man to keep half a dozen arrows

stuck into the ground beside him. A skilled archer, after shooting his first arrow, could follow it with five more before the first had reached the target.

In shooting, the archer did not draw back the string. He held the arrow, on the string, by his right ear, and thrust the bowstave away with his left hand. His whole body was thrown into the movement. Though this required

[85]

a high degree of wiry strength and activity, it must have been repeated in rapid time. French chroniclers of the period recorded that the sky was darkened by the flying showers of arrows.

There was more to the arrow storm than mere appearance. It was said that the clothyard shaft, flighted with grey goose or turkey feathers, could pierce plate armour at 200 yards.

In this way the foot-soldier was re-established as an important entity, working in co-operation with the cavalry. When the archer had broken the force of the enemy's charge, the cavalry protected him from attack by those who did reach the position. Mounted troops of the 14th century were not all knights. Quite often a knight was called upon for a larger number of mounted men than he could find at short notice. He would then equip his sons and some serving men as *servientes eques*, mounted sergeants.

Early in the century, inferior mounted troops were re-named *squires*, and were often referred to as *men-at-arms*. They were armed and armoured like knights, without the latters' golden spurs. *Esquires* held an entirely different position, as apprentices attendant upon knights, with the prospect of being knighted if they proved worthy. In general, army mounts were still heavy and clumsy. Possibly this was one reason for the low standard of horsemanship in England. Other drawbacks were the poorly designed bridles, with unsuitable bits, and the encumbered rider himself. Spanish horses were the most popular, but they were not common in England.

When serving on a campaign, the knight had four horses —two for riding in battle, a palfrey for travel, and a packhorse for baggage. His battle horses were led by his esquire, and the horse that he normally used in action was led on the right of the esquire. For this reason, it became known as the *dextratius* (from the Latin *dexter* = right), which name became corrupted into *destrier*.

Cavalry and archers chiefly composed the army of Edward III of England when he landed at St Vaast-la-Hague in July, 1346. Edward had in all 32,000 men, and he had seen to it that they were well trained and organized. One result of the Crusades had been increased trade with the East, bringing a larger amount of money into circulation. Soldiers were then able to draw regular scales of pay. This raised the humbler men from the level of serfs, and provided a little money by the end of the campaign.

In spite of his vital importance, the archer was only paid threepence a day, though this was doubled if he was mounted and able to ride to battle. Mounted men were always better paid. A knight's pay was two shillings a day (eight times as much as an archer), and men at arms received one shilling.

There were two other classes of mounted men. Next in rank to the men at arms were *pauncenors* (a corruption of the German *panzer*, armour), at sixpence a day. These men wore *haubergeons* and carried lances. Lowest in the cavalry scale were the *hobelars*, so named from the hobbies or rough ponies that they rode. The *hobelars* were skirmishers, with *hacketons* (quilted coats), helmets, and swords. Like the *pauncenors*, their pay was sixpence a day.

It is a curious thing that the soldiers who received the least pay—Welsh spearmen, at twopence a day—were the first uniformly-clad troops in the English army. They had been issued with tunics and mantles by the King.

All these troops, though well-trained, were of orthodox type, but Edward had in his forces a number of soldiers whose duties were entirely new. The King's father, Edward II (1307–27) was recorded as having used "crack-eyes of war" against the Scots, but the third Edward had a developed form of this arm.

[87]

Here they are with their devilish engines, both men and gear foul and blackened. "Gonnes," they are called, and chancy things to deal with. See how the men take out a section of the thick, iron tube that lies roped down on its carved-out wooden bed. Into the freed section of the tube,

GUNNERS, MID-14TH CENTURY.

which section has a blocked-up end, the men shovel some black powder and wad it in with tow. Next, a ball of stone, likewise stuffed in with tow, and the piece is returned to its place at the back end of the tube. A great wedge is driven in behind it, and, Lord save us, one man takes fire to put to the thing. There is a noise such as one never heard, and we are all whelmed in black, stinging smoke, with a flash of fire before us.

Gunners—men who chose to risk maiming and death in

[88]

the service of the infernal weapon. They were incredibly highly paid for foot-soldiers—a shilling a day—but everyone regarded them and their devices with unease. The men themselves, conscious of their superiority, lorded it a little over their fellow soldiers, and tended to hold aloof in their company.

It was indeed a dangerous service. Both guns and powder were unpredictable as regards strength, and bursting was not uncommon. In general, the effect of early gunfire was moral rather than physical; chroniclers wrote of the guns "which, with fire, threw little iron balls to frighten the horses." If the position was overrun, the guns were abandoned, for they had no wheels; they were transported on oxcarts. However, without carts the enemy could not get the guns away, so they might be recaptured.

On the battlefield of Crécy, apparently the first big engagement featuring guns, Edward's army numbered 18,000 men. Drawn up before them was a large French force including 10,000 knights, 15,000 Genoese crossbowmen, 20,000 skirmishers, and several corps of militia. It was a badly co-ordinated army, the product of successive ideas for the creation of a national force.

There was always difficulty in raising a well-knit force in France. The basic cavalry unit was a small group known as a *lance*: the knight, with squires and armsbearers, six men in all. This group varied in strength where a large escort was brought to the muster, and in such cases there was wrangling over precedence on the march. Each community was bound to provide a set number of troops, which differed greatly in quality. Some towns contributed *trained bands*, professional soldiers who were valuable when competently led, but at the other end of the scale was a mere rabble.

As always in the Middle Ages, there was little provision for the welfare of the soldier. However, we must remember that the majority of the troops were peasants, whose normal way of life was comfortless.

When the French army reached the scene of action at Crécy, the foot-soldiers were in poor shape. After an unorganized march of eighteen miles through heavy rain, all were tired and dispirited, "and," says the record, "neither the king nor the marshals were masters of their men." The militia of Caen had already met the invaders, and Jean Froissart, a French chronicler, wrote of the militia: "As soon as the burgesses saw the English advancing in three battles, in close and powerful array, perceived their pennons, and heard the roar of those archers ... they were so dismayed that no man in the world could have stayed them from flight."

In this unencouraging situation, defeat was in every man's mind. At length the Genoese were directed to open the action, though their crossbow cords were relaxed through becoming wet (a crossbow could not be unstrung like a longbow). Though the Genoese raised a gallant shout, designed to strike terror into the English, it was without effect. Stepping forward, the longbowmen poured upon them such a devastating arrow-storm that the wretched Genoese broke up and retreated pell-mell.

Utter confusion followed; the French king, infuriated by the sight, ordered his cavalry to advance and ride down the rabble on the way. This was attempted, but neither armour nor courage could face the deadly hail. In two hours the English had the field.

Even in later years, it seemed that the French soldier could never gain the needful cohesion with his fellows; the bond of common purpose was not there. At Poitiers, in 1356, the French knights made futile efforts to dislodge the English from their hill position. When they had sent their horses to the rear, owing to the horses' fear of gunfire, the Frenchmen attempted the hill on foot. A charge by the English cavalry beat them to the ground, and King John was captured.

The effect of this setback was frightful. Throughout the country, dire confusion reigned. Bands of rebellious peasants, known as *Jacquerie*, roved the land, burning chateaux and hanging their owners. Contending factions laid waste the countryside for years, and even after the English had withdrawn there were still powerful armed bands for the authorities to quell.

With the opening of the 15th century the dreary tale of reverses began again. At Agincourt, in 1415, the flower of French nobility went down before the terrible archers in a new English invasion. Insufficient reconnaissance and general mismanagement brought utter defeat. The French cavalry attempted to charge over broken, muddy ground against archers esconced behind a hedge of oblique pointed stakes. Ten thousand men were lost, chiefly of the aristocracy, whereas the English losses did not exceed two score.

These resounding victories caused a great change in other nations' opinion of the English. European writers commented on the rise of this "most warlike nation" (1360). "The natives are bold and hardy, renowned in arms and victorious in war" (1400).

An upsurge of French national spirit was the welcome change that swept over the country a few years after the death of the English King Henry V, in 1422. This great patriotic movement was given heart by the French national heroine, Jeanne d'Arc, the "Maid of Orleans."

The girl herself was of peasant stock. She was born in 1411, in the little village of Domrémy, midway between Champagne and Lorraine. Jeanne and her compatriots were convinced that she personified the prophesied virgin who should come from Domrémy forest to liberate France.

In 1429, the Dauphin Charles was persuaded by popular feeling to give audience to the peasant girl, and she convinced him of her mission. In spite of the romantic stories that have crowded around her name, Jeanne was not particularly good-looking, though kindly and agreeable. She was illiterate, and there does not seem to have been any military genius in her leadership of the French forces,

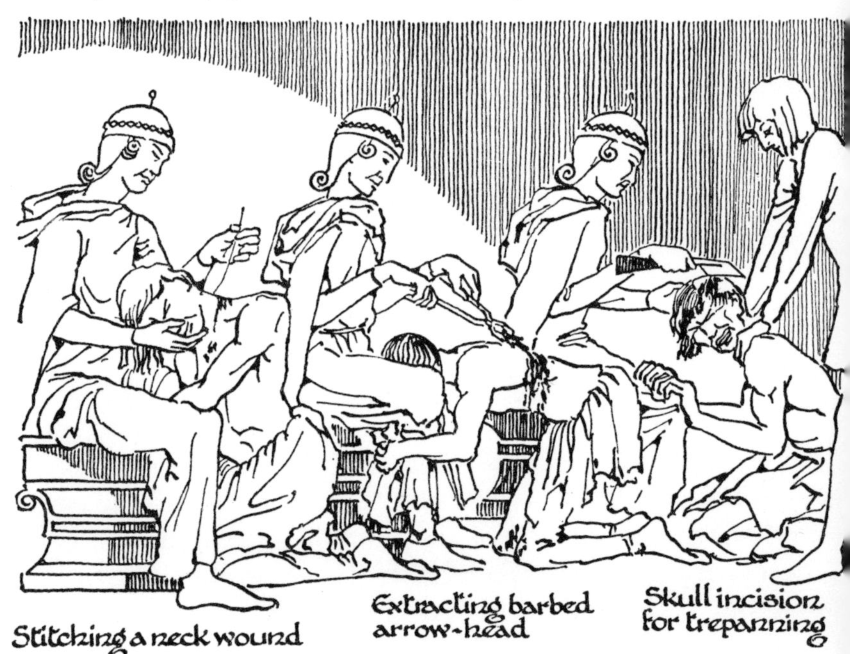

EARLY MEDIÆVAL SURGERY
Based on 13th century MS O.1.20, Trin. Coll., Camb.

but she provided a much-needed spirit of resolution. Both friends and enemies regarded her with superstitious awe, and the troops developed fanatical enthusiasm. Jeanne's personal white standard, her white (polished) armour, and her ancient sword, of supposedly mystical origin, spurred the troops to immense efforts.

The female warrior was finally captured at the siege of Compiègne, in May, 1429, through an ill-judged sortie against the English. She was burnt after a perfidious trial as a sorceress, but her name still holds magic for the French.

[92]

8. With Pike and Handgun

In spite of the depressing series of events that opened the 15th century in France, redemption emerged from defeat. A dedicated zeal, which survived the death of Jeanne d'Arc, urged the French soldier to maintain the struggle that she had begun. In spite of the weak and vacillating king, Charles VII (1422–61) the Orleans Ordinance for a standing army was established in 1439. This decree was really implemented, unlike previous futile efforts. Probably it was due to a minor revolution in the royal councils, which resulted in the inclusion of commoners to form a majority.

One of the first moves was to organize a cavalry force. It consisted of fifteen companies of *gendarmerie*, each of a hundred lances. In this case each lance comprised one man at arms, three bowmen, a spearman, and a page, all armed and mounted. In all, the cavalry force numbered 9,000 men.

There was a similar rearrangement of infantry. Feudal troops were largely replaced by companies of paid cross-bowmen, pikemen, and gunners. Though the French were slow to appreciate the value of cannon, which were quite formidable by that time, they developed the arm with perseverance. Having at last established an ordered military force, they mounted a series of determined actions that pushed back the English invader. By 1453, the latter held only Calais.

Through her sweeping reorganization, France then possessed the first standing army of professional soldiers in Europe. Her cavalry was divided into three sections. First came the *gendarmerie*, equipped with costly Milan armour and twelve-foot lances. Light cavalry formed the next division. These men were known as *reîtres*, as the type of soldier was of German origin, they had breast-plates and short lances. In the third cavalry section, the scouts, there was a new departure—the mounted hand-gunner. A proportion of the men had small cannon, of about half-inch bore, suspended by a ring around the neck. This weapon was simply an iron tube fixed to a stock, with a loop at the end of the stock.

Handguns had been used among European foot-soldiers since about 1360, and this service called for an intrepid type of man. At that date, field cannon were still a novelty, and it took a high degree of courage to volunteer for service as a handgunner. As with the field gun, little damage was done in the early days, but a Milanese writer, Biblius, reported that handgunners at Lucca, in 1430, inflicted

[94]

great loss on a besieging force. Bembo of Venice, writing in 1490, commented on the introduction of handguns "transmitted to us from Germany." He recorded that the Venetian Council of Ten recruited instructors for dispatch to various towns. Every village was required to have two

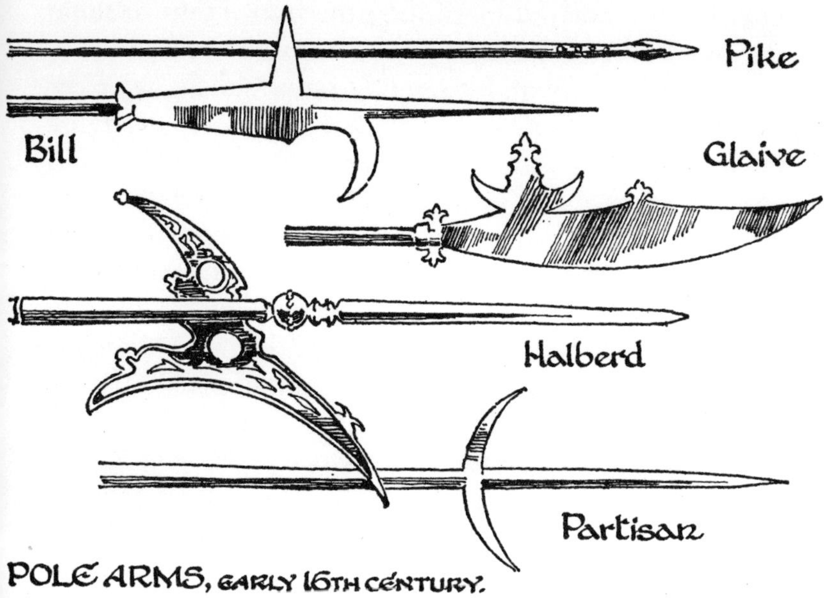

POLE ARMS, EARLY 16TH CENTURY.

men specializing in handguns, who would be freed of other public obligations. Annual shoots were directed, the prize being a year's freedom from public service for the winner's community.

Even after the establishment of a standing force, there was a long transitional period before the French achieved a regular, permanent army. It was always easy to bring in foreign mercenaries, and powerful lords often did this to further their own schemes. By the end of the 15th century, the European military scene was greatly changed through this practice. Infantry had regained prime importance; the developing handgun (*arquebus*), the bow, and the pike, fifteen to eighteen feet long, made a powerful combination.

Swiss and German mercenaries were commonly found in France. The former were famous for their effective use of the pike *en masse*. When they were drawn up to repel cavalry, the foremost ranks presented a bristling *hedgehog*. It was achieved by drilling the front ranks to slope the pike forward at an angle, with a rigid hold and the butt under the instep. Succeeding ranks did the same, in staggered formation, to present a formidable barrier of points.

If an advance was ordered, the pikemen brought their weapons to the *charge*—a horizontal position, with the butt in the right hand, at arm's length behind, and the left hand forward at full stretch, shoulder high. The whole mass of men then advanced slowly like the classical phalanx, to win their objective "by push of pike."

A pikeman was chosen for his height and length of limb. Swiss were preferred for their extreme bravery and toughness. The average Swiss pikeman was a thoroughly reliable soldier, not easily dismayed, and amenable to discipline. His only flaw was that on occasion he might become temperamental.

Pike-hedge and missile weapon between them restored infantry to the place of power. The idea of massed points as a protection against cavalry had appeared earlier in the Middle Ages. During the reign of Edward I, Nicholas Trivet recorded the use of a defensive spear circle by Welsh irregulars. The Scots tried a massed spear technique, as well, but these primitive formations were unsuitable for movement.

Military organization of the French type was general throughout Europe by the early 16th century. It is difficult, however, to treat the German soldier separately from the French, through the effect of the mercenary system.

[96]

Many German princes carried on a regular industry by raising and training soldiers for hire. These *landsknechte* were spirited and willing in service, but they lived up to their title as mercenaries. There was a continual demand for increased pay, and they were rapacious plunderers.

GERMAN MERCENARIES, 16TH CENTURY.

On at least one occasion, *landsknechte* of Charles VII were guilty of an atrocious crime. Charles invaded Italy in 1494, and the town of Pontremé surrendered without trouble. However, some of the townsmen apparently quarrelled with the mercenaries, who killed every man in sight, and raised a disastrous fire that destroyed the food supply. Philip de Commines wrote that, to gain pardon, the Germans manhandled the fourteen-gun artillery train over the Apennines.

An important item in French reorganization was the permanent grouping of soldiers into companies and regiments for administration. Infantry were directed in battalions (from *battaglia*, battle array), and the tactical unit for cavalry was the squadron (Italian *squadrone*, square).

Francis I of France (1515–47) was one of the European monarchs who issued "Articles of War," i.e., a set of regulations governing the soldier's conduct and imposing penalties for breaches of them. He formed seven "territorial legions" in 1534, broadly based on the Roman unit, with each legion 6,000 strong. Though chiefly composed of pikemen, the legions included arquebusiers, and a number of halberdiers were provided for close action. The halberd was a spiked axe on a long pole. Pikemen in the front ranks were armoured to the knees, but the remainder were "bare pikes," relying upon weapon numbers and close formation for protection.

Originally, the battalion resembled one of these legions, and contained several regiments. These troops would be in close formation, so that one man's voice could command the 500 or 600 in a company. Changes in weapons brought an extended formation, so the situation became reversed— a battalion, reduced in numbers, was part of a regiment.

Quite early in the 16th century, there was a regular issue of firearms to some cavalry units, where previously the lance alone had been employed. The cavalryman received wheel-lock pistols, discharged by sparks created between a serrated wheel and a piece of iron pyrites. Ammunition was supplied in the form of measured charges of powder, each wrapped with a bullet in a piece of coarse paper. By the middle of the century these charges were carried in a small box with holes, called a *patron*.

[98]

Notorious among the early 16th-century cavalry were the German horse pistoliers, mercenaries known by the old name of *Reiters*. These riders attacked in the manner of the oldtime charioteers, by riding up to the embattled footmen, firing their pistols, and wheeling off to reload. Though the tactics were basically unsound, to ride along the front of an unbroken enemy, the discharges had considerable effect on morale.

The *Reiters* themselves were of the worst type as regards conduct. In action they were fearless, but in victory they spread horror and devastation through a captured town. A sight of their blackened faces—a feature of the Reiters' battle array—foretold an orgy of murder and senseless destruction.

Cavalry horses of this period were of much better type than the old mediaeval war horses. Through the Moors' occupation of Spain (ended 1492) an infusion of Arab blood in the stock had produced a lighter, faster strain. It is true that horsemanship was still in its infancy, because of poor saddlery and bits, and Spanish or Italian riders were considered the best in Europe. Though firing from the saddle was a common practice, there can have been little accuracy.

As the use of firearms developed, the medical profession was confronted with the treatment of gunshot wounds. At that time, a great deal of so-called medical science was absolute mumbo jumbo, as one may see by reading 16th-century literature on the subject. This resulted in excruciating torture for the patient; in fact, it was considered by some pessimists that any bullet wound meant death at the hands of the surgeons. Probably this was an exaggeration, though the earliest treatment gives it credence. A hole made by a crude lead ball had often a blackish rim, stained by the lead. The surgeons read in this signs of blood poisoning, so the wound was cauterized with a red-hot iron. It

[99]

was not considered suitable to apply the mediaeval salve of warm pitch.

In extracting a bullet, if it was not deep-seated, a cross was cut in the flesh, and the missile was squeezed out. For deeper wounds, crude probes were employed, a source of infection that probably gave rise to the high death rate.

In the reconstituted armies of Europe, most men were volunteers; levies were only raised at times of stress. It was usual for the ruler to make a contract with a nobleman—who was noted for his military service or his wealth—to raise a regiment in return for a down payment and annual maintenance. Captains were engaged by the commander; some might bring companies with them. There was regular supervision of the regiments, through periodical musters called by royal commissaries. These officers saw to it that the commander was doing his duty, and they issued to him the pay and subsistence expenses of his force.

It seems that the 16th-century soldier paid for at least part of his food—probably all. A petition to the Privy Council of Mary I of England complained of the high cost of living through scarcity: "... the soldiers are not able to live of their accustomed wages."

In that year (1557) cavalry were paid ninepence a day and foot-soldiers sixpence, so in consequence of the plea, they were allotted an extra threepence and twopence each respectively every payday "in reward" to offset the price of wheat, etc. Officers were granted "rewards" on the same schedule; one of the officers was styled "Petty captain"—evidently an early term for lieutenant.

The English army of the mid-16th century is shown in great detail in a series of seven drawings housed in the British Museum. Among the troops depicted are companies of archers, typically English, for no Continental army had the longbow as a standard infantry weapon.

[100]

Crossbows had long been banned in England to foster use of the longbow, and Henry VIII was against handguns for the same reason when he became king in 1509.

A useful comparison can be drawn from the picture showing the English opposed to a Continental army. Scout cavalry is skirmishing in the terrain between the forces. Each section of English pikes and halberdiers is preceded and followed by three ranks of arquebusiers; detachments of archers guard the flanks, and on the wings are squadrons of heavy cavalry.

Presumably the other army is French. It shows no archers, and the pikemen are enclosed by ranks of arquebusiers on front, rear, and flanks. Otherwise the disposition is much the same. We may see by this that the English, while retaining the longbow, followed the Continental practice of fielding a fair number of arquebusiers.

In another picture of the series, an English army is shown on the march, in disciplined order—scouts, cavalry wings, front, rear, and flank units of arquebusiers, and the artillery train. Bringing up the rear is the domestic unit—female camp followers, baggage and provision wagons, and ration livestock. This drawing is inscribed "King Henry the eights Army."

An excellent example of training is shown in the fifth drawing of the series. In this, the flanking arquebusiers advance in ranks beyond the pikes to fire in turn. Each rank, after firing, turns around and countermarches to the rear between the files, reloading while on the move.

These pictures show that most foot-soldiers of the period (about 1540) wore the doublet and hose of everyday life, without protection. It had been perceived that, in facing gunfire, a wound was more readily located for "treatment" if no armour covered it.

There was a variety of headgear, two or three types of headpiece, or a simple flat cap for the majority. Officers frequently wore broad, heavily-plumed hats, and ornately-slashed and embellished garments. English and European armies were the same in these respects, but English troops were distinguished by the Tudor green and white, white coats with the red cross, and the St. George's banner.

VOLUNTEER, LONDON TRAINED BANDS.
1539.

During the reign in question, the London trained bands drew great attention by their standard of training and organization. When the men paraded before the King at Mile End, in 1539, they displayed within their ranks the military changes of the times. Marching in three divisions,

[102]

preceded by horse-drawn artillery and the city's flags, the white-clad unpaid soldiers presented five ranks of arquebusiers leading each division. Archers, pikemen, and billmen followed in that order, so that handguns, bows, and pikes made their first recorded appearance together in English history. This muster was typical of the forces ready to hand all over England—men who had equipped themselves at their own charges, and who gave their time freely to provide for the country's protection.

As the King's personal guard, there existed the unit raised in his father's time. After the turmoil of civil war, it was felt that a standing force should be provided for the sovereign's protection. In 1485 the Yeomen of the Guard were instituted as a Royal bodyguard, and this famous unit is still in being. Its duties have always been carried out in London, and the scarlet, gold, and black uniform, with the Tudor rose charged on it, still bears some resemblance to the original.

Throughout the 16th century, England was in danger of attack, so the sovereign had always to be ready to mobilize forces. Some documents of the latter part of the century make quaint reading on this score. For instance, in May 1588, before the Armada's coming, the Earl of Huntingdon wrote to Sir William Fairfax: "It is thought sufficient for the first three days' training to give every shot"—arquebusier—"one pound of powder and a quarter of a pound of match"—slow-match—to fire the matchlock gun—"because the most men know not how to use their pieces, and therefore to train them with false fires at first is thought most fit."

In the following year, an order was sent to Deputy Lieutenants of counties advising them to accept substitutes for wealthy men, farmers and householders, who had been called to the army. The authorities commented that though these were the people who could best afford to provide their kit, they were least able, through soft living, to bear the hardships of service.

A bitter complaint of the same period concerned soldiers going to muster "who very disorderly refused to wear and carry their armour and other warlike furniture from the towns where they dwell. . . ." Other people, such as constables, were forced to transport the men's gear. It was decreed, therefore, that soldiers going to muster should receive, as an extra to their eightpence a day in wages, a penny a mile to carry their equipment, for a maximum of six miles. If a man still refused, he was liable to lose all his pay, and be jailed for four days.

Some idea of service kit at that time may be seen in the list of clothing for the Irish campaign at the end of the century. This comprised a canvas doublet, a pair of broadcloth Venetians (breeches), two shirts and two bands (collars), a pair of shoes and two pairs of brogues (heavy shoes), three pair of stockings, a "hat cap," a long broadcloth cassock, lined, or an Irish mantle. Stoppages for these articles accounted for over half the soldier's pay.

When the Spanish invasion threatened, there was a general call to arms, especially around the south coast of England. In each district, the resident gentry were given command of units formed among local workers, with pike and handgun. There were three classes of handgun in use —the old-type arquebus and the new caliver, both of which could be fired from the shoulder without much difficulty, and the musket, a long, heavy gun of Spanish origin, which was fired from a forked rest or crutch. It carried a lead ball of twelve to the pound, while the other two guns used balls of sixteen to the pound.

Evidently some arms-training was still faulty; an instruction of the late 16th century condemned the practice of firing as a whole unit together. The writer showed that this mass discharge "only serves to make a great crack." He said that the rear ranks risked shooting the ranks before them, or firing so high as to waste their shots. Details were given of firing by rank, as specified in the account of Henry VIII's army.

Until about 1550, Englishmen regarded the Scottish clansman as a wild half-brigand rather than a soldier, but from that date onward the Scots pikemen were undoubtedly the best in the British Isles. There were few firearms among them, but they were equipped with sword, buckler (a small shield) and dagger besides the pike. Where other pikes were protected with plate to the knees, the Scots wore only an iron "skull" and a *jack* (a knee-length reinforced garment) with a kerchief wound twice around the neck. In advancing, they kept close order in ranks, with their points crossed and bucklers on their left arms.

Scots pikes saw a great deal of action in France, where for centuries the kings had maintained the *Garde Ecossais*, which later became the Scots Guards of the British Army.

9. 17th-Century English Soldiers

Just as the archer was the key man of the mediaeval army, the musketeer in his turn became of prime importance. In Henry VIII's army handguns had been in the minority, but at the end of the 16th century, the Dutch prince Maurice of Nassau fielded shot and pikes in equal proportion. A battalion of 500 men comprised pikemen ten ranks deep in the centre, with files of musketeers on the flanks. Musketeers could each fire a shot every two minutes; theoretically, gunfire broke up the charge and pikes kept off those horsemen who reached the defensive position.

A musketeer's equipment of the early 17th century has been made familiar by the work of Jacob de Gheyn, whose *Wapenhandelinghe* (Exercise of Arms) was published in Antwerp in 1608. His drawings have often appeared in history books under such titles as "A musketeer of James I," but of course the drawings show *Dutch* soldiers.

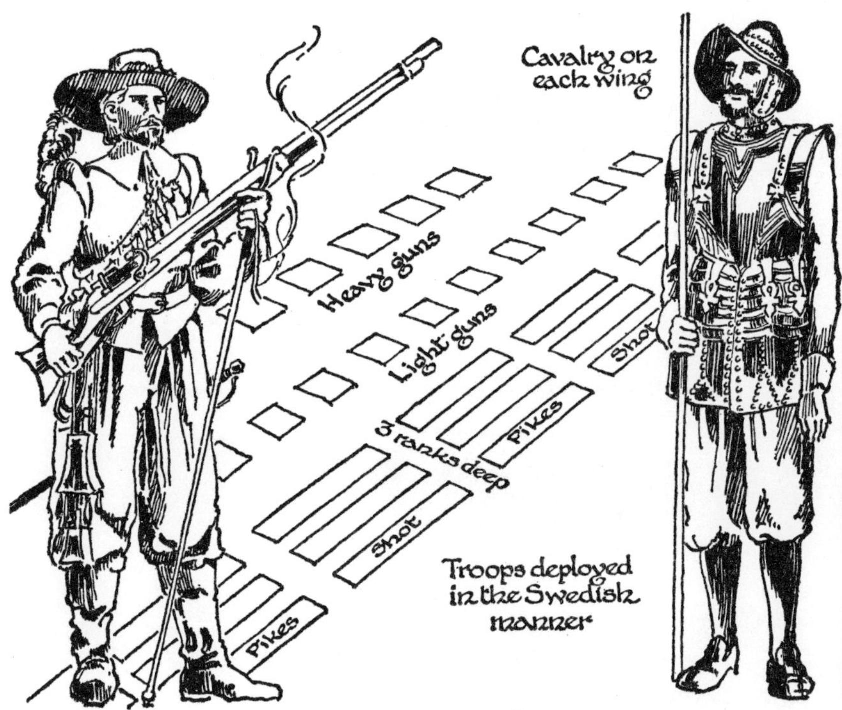

BRITISH BATTLE ORDER, 1620.

There were a number of accessories for the service of the firearm. Across the musketeer's chest, from left to right, was slung a "collar of bandoliers." It was a broad leather belt suspending a dozen wooden bottles, each of which contained a measured charge of powder. The soldier called his bottles the Twelve Apostles. By his right hip hung a bag of bullets, and on long cords below that

[108]

was a square powder flask, with a spring-lever stopper, for refilling the bandoliers. In a small "priming flask," hanging below the other flask, was a quantity of fine powder for the priming-pan of the musket. This priming was set

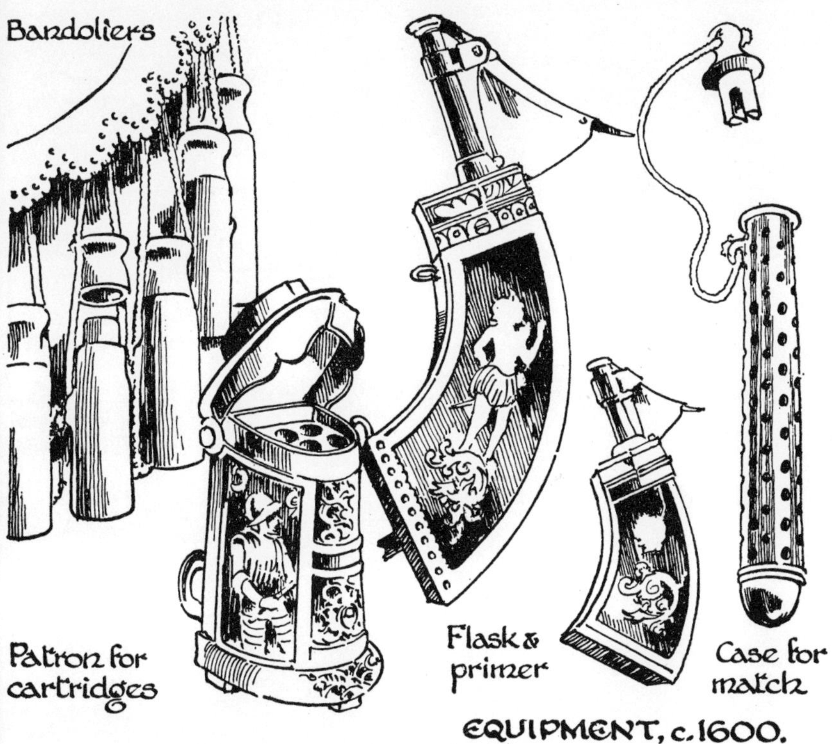

EQUIPMENT, c. 1600.

off by the lighted matchcord fixed in the cock of the musket, and the explosion was communicated to the charge through the touchhole.

A loop of spare matchcord was carried with the flasks, but the piece of match to be actually in the musket lock for firing was kept, alight at both ends, between the second and third fingers of the left hand. On occasion, a *matchcase* was carried, a perforated tube in which the match could be placed to keep it alight. There was never a flame on

[109]

the match; it glowed like the end of a cigar when it was blown upon, or whirled around.

Dutch, Spanish, and English muskets were of the same general design, the butt being almost in line with the barrel. The French preferred a curved stock, which made

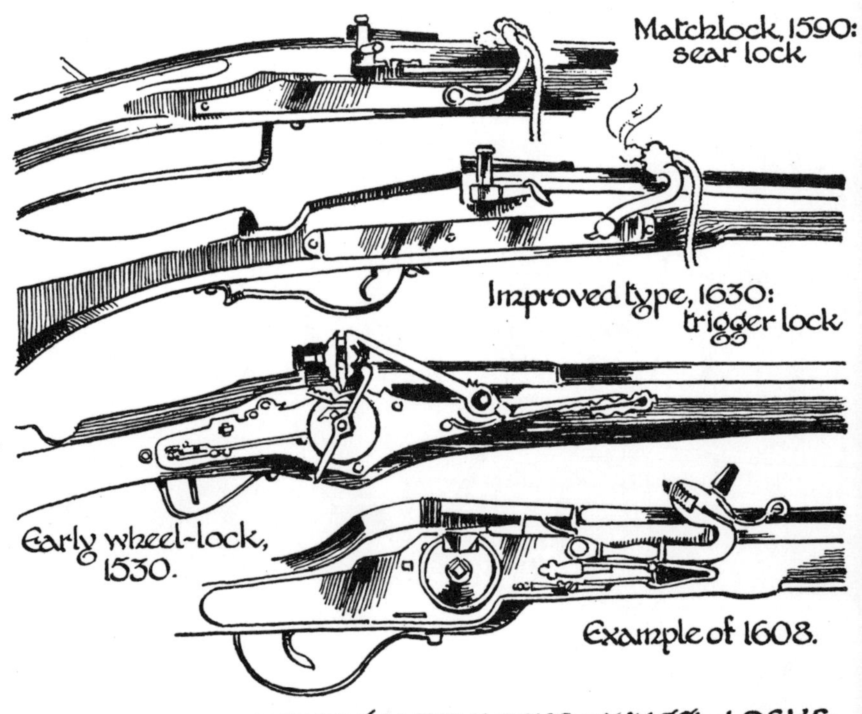

SERVICE MATCHLOCKS & WHEEL-LOCKS.

the recoil difficult to withstand. A musket might weigh sixteen pounds or more—when the original heavy type was introduced from Spain it took two men to handle it— so a U-headed crutch was used when taking aim.

Arms manuals of that period give over thirty drill movements for loading and firing. Some of the directions are curiously expressed, e.g., after priming "Blow off your loose corns"—loose powder around the priming pan. Gunpowder was chiefly made up into grains—*corned* powder—to maintain its consistency and give better ignition than the old dustlike powder.

When the musketeer was in action, he put two or three bullets into his mouth to speed up loading. This practice produced a ring of black around his mouth by the time firing had ceased. After emptying a bandolier down the barrel and ramming down wadding with his "scouring stick," he spat down a bullet and wadded that. A supply of wadding, tow or rag, was kept in the hatband.

Jacob de Gheyn's drawings show the caliverman wearing a high rounded helmet called a *cabacete*, while the musketeer wore a broad, feathered hat. The rest of his clothing was normal wear for a soldier—ordinary civilian doublet, baggy breeches, stockings, and shoes or short boots. English musketeers frequently wore red breeches as a distinguishing feature.

Firearms were bringing about a considerable change in the structure of English and Continental armies. English military archery was officially abolished in 1595, when the Privy Council ordered that all trained bands should be armed only with arquebuses, calivers, and muskets. Cavalrymen had already exchanged the lance for the pistol, and sometimes a carbine was added, carrying a ball of thirty to the pound.

It was not practical for a horseman to wear a rattling collar of bandoliers, so the patron of *cartouches* or paper packets with charges was still in use. A great advantage of this form of loading was that the soldier simply bit off the end of the *cartouche*, poured the powder down the barrel, and rammed down the paper with the bullet, wadding the whole charge at once.

One or two 17th-century writers strongly urged the issue of patrons to musketeers. Edward Davies (*England's Trainings*, 1619) remarked that Low Countries levies, in Flanders, Holland, etc., used bandoliers, the Spaniards used the flask, the French soldier both methods, and some English troops their pockets! Another authority commented on the drawbacks of bandoliers in night actions or ambushes, where their clattering betrayed the wearers.

Davis' advice to the soldier on selecting a musket was illuminating.

"Make choice of a Milan peece, for they be of tough and perfect temper, light, square, and bigge of breech, and very strong where the powder doth lie, and where the violent force of the powder doth consist, and notwithstanding thinne at the end. Our English peeces approach very neare to them in goodness and beautie (their heaviness only excepted)."

At that time infantry had been classified in two main groups as to arms and physical types. As before, height and length of limb were important for the pikeman, as well as strength, so that he could control the immense length of the pike—sixteen to eighteen feet in the 17th century. Matters were reversed in the missile section—the musketeer was chosen short and stockily built, with stout legs, to endure the shock of the recoil. This was a considerable factor in training recruits—poor butt design, lack of balance, and excessive length of barrel made the musket unhandy, apart from the actual firing. In close action, the men were encouraged to club the musket and lay about them.

The old system of recruitment, with gentry as officers, was officially abandoned at the beginning of the century, and bodies of militia were formed, chiefly on a voluntary basis. Recruits were initially trained in musketry by easy stages. First they flashed a little powder in the priming pan, and when that was familiar a small charge of powder was loaded and fired. This charge was increased each time until the full loaded charge was reached—a development of the Earl of Huntingdon's "false fires."

There was a grave decline in the standard of training during the reign of Charles I (1625–49). Militiamen were called out for exercise only once in five years. London regiments kept up regular training, and these were good troops. Throughout the rest of the country, few militiamen could load their muskets competently, and many men were afraid to fire a shotted charge. Provincial regiments were undisciplined through the inefficiency of their commanders; they were poorly provided with kit and arms, and a generally mutinous spirit prevailed.

Early in his reign, the King had antagonized the public by trying to maintain a standing army to help his brother-in-law in Germany. Charles raised an army of 10,000 men by forced loans, and illegally billeted them on the public. These troops were disorderly, and the King resorted to martial law—another illegal practice in peacetime. The outcome of this was the Petition of Right, which curbed the King's activities.

This was the situation when Charles' inept handling of Scottish affairs brought the latter into active rebellion over the attempted imposition of the new Prayer Book. At the same time, the King was trying to gain from Parliament a grant of money for fighting the Scots. During August 1640, a Scottish invasion force fought its way across the Tyne and occupied an area reaching to the north bank of the Tees.

In extremity, Charles revived the ancient feudal levy, and mustered the militia, but without achieving an army worth calling by the name. He was forced to recall the Parliament that he had dismissed, to get money to buy off the invaders. At the new election, a great majority of Puritans, the King's enemies, gained seats. After a series of shrewd moves in Parliament, and ill-advised activities by the King, the two factions resorted to arms in 1642.

On the first battlefield of the Civil War, Edgehill, in

north Oxfordshire, both armies were amateurs. King and Parliament had each called up their adherents, to make soldiers of them as best they might. On each side were some experienced officers, and the King's gentlemen were skilled in the saddle and in arms. These supporters of the Crown were chiefly from the north and the south-west, and they brought with them retainers and tenants to go into the infantry. The men were equipped for war at their masters' charges.

Puritan supporters were culled from farming, trading, and industrial areas. Many of the men had to start from scratch in the business of becoming soldiers, but Parliament held the national purse, so funds were forthcoming to equip an army. It is true that both parties soon took over the arsenals of the useless militia.

As there was no national army, there was no uniform. At Edgehill, the Royalists wore white scarves, and their opponents orange scarves. At a later stage of the war, blue was accepted as the Royal hue, and red was that of the Parliamentarians.

That first pitched battle taught lessons to both sides. For instance, Prince Rupert, the King's nephew, was a soldier of towering spirit and high courage. He headed the Royal cavalry in a charge that carried the weak opposing horsemen right off the field, but he maintained an undisciplined pursuit. This left the Royal infantry exposed to attack from the Parliamentary foot and the remaining cavalry.

When at last Rupert's force returned, blown horses and weary riders, their infantry had been battling against heavy odds for several hours. Night came, to close the action. Though both armies claimed victory, there was nothing to choose between them, save that the King's troops had lost most men through the desperate infantry stand.

The cavalry actions of later battles showed a complete contrast between the two armies' tactics. Rupert, who at twenty-three had seen much action on the Continent, was a dashing horseman. He favoured the charge home at top speed, and he introduced the use of the pistol as a preliminary. It seems likely that only the front rank fired before going in with the sword, the other ranks following without firing. This would save the majority of the pistols for the pursuit; the normal procedure.

In the Edgehill combat, Oliver Cromwell, a Huntingdon farmer, had commanded a troop of cavalry. He noted the defects of both armies' shock troops—wild, uncontrolled charges on one side, feeble, ill-trained clods on the other. When he made his way to power, he instituted a drill for charging at a trot, an advance resembling the old "push of pike".

Cromwell's most important move for the Parliamentary cause was to push on the reorganization of the forces into his "New Model Army." This was designed to be a professional combat force, trained and equipped in the best manner. The men themselves were physically fit and hardy, so much so that they earned the name of *Ironsides*. Their coats were red, with their respective colonels' colours as facings.

At that date (1644) there was a strange disparity between the weekly pay of an infantryman (3s. 6d.) and a trooper of cavalry (10s. 0d.). In fact, the foot-soldier's pay was the same as in 1557. There was a considerable difference throughout the entire pay scale of the respective units—captains, for instance, received £2 10s. in the infantry but £5 in the cavalry. Officers provided their own clothing and equipment, but other ranks suffered pay stoppages for kit issue.

In the New Model Army discipline was extremely severe. For cases of blasphemy, the penalty was a hot iron

[115]

through the tongue. Swearing was punished by loss of pay and other impositions, and there was a painful ordeal for the drunkard. It was the *wooden horse*, a long triangular block fixed horizontally on legs, with a sharp edge uppermost. On this the offender sat for an hour a day, on several successive days. Liquor cans were hung around his neck, and muskets to a maximum number of three were tied to each foot to increase his weight upon the edge.

This list of misdeeds may sound strange for a Puritan army, wherein a soldier was fined a penny if he did not attend the daily prayers. Would such godly men drink to excess, and blaspheme?

In fact, the Parliamentary troops were led by Puritans, and many were in the ranks, but a large number of the troops were nothing but tongue-in-cheek Puritans, hoping for pickings through the upheaval of the country. However, it was this highly-trained army that ground down the Royalist effort, and later provided Cromwell with his weapon of power.

During our study of army units, we have seen little of the men behind the big guns. There is good reason for this. Artillery was an unorganized section of the army, with no regular establishment. Civilian drivers were employed for the gun teams, which might include over twenty horses in a single team. Big siege pieces like the *cannon*, throwing a 60 pound ball, needed twenty-three horses to transport them, for the gun and carriage weighed three tons. A 16-pounder *culverin* weighed a ton, and had a team of nine horses, with proportionately smaller teams for 9-pounder and 6-pounder field guns.

In Cromwell's new army there was a regular siege train of 60-pounders and *demi-cannon* (32-pounders), beside 12-inch mortars throwing spherical cast-iron shells of that diameter. There were fifty-six siege cannon and a similar number of field guns, 9-pounders and lesser pieces.

Artillery personnel included two special units, an escort of two regiments of infantry, and a company of pioneers, who dug and prepared gun emplacements. The escort was issued with flintlock muskets, to avoid bringing a number of burning matches near the artillery powder supply. In

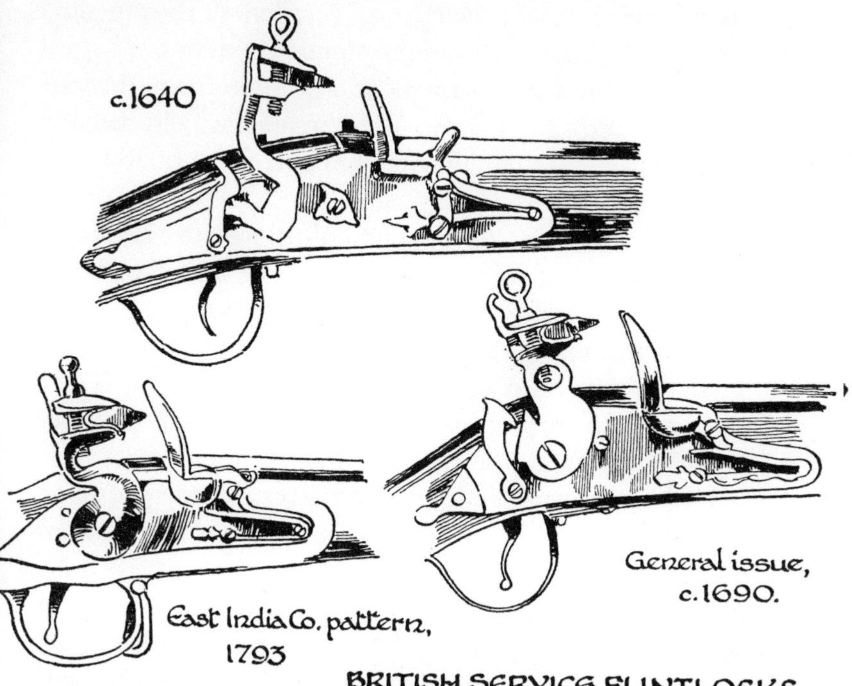

the flintlock, a spring-loaded cock held a shaped piece of flint in its jaws. When the trigger was pressed, the flint was driven hard against the steel on the priming pan cover, producing sparks which fired the priming and thus led fire through the touchhole to the main charge. Our illustration shows stages in the development of flintlock types.

Originally the New Model Army consisted of infantry and cavalry totalling 21,000 men, in proportion of about two to one respectively, besides 1,000 *dragoons*. The latter troops, first mentioned about 1600, were like the old-time mounted infantry, using horses simply as transport to the field. Dragoons were armed with carbines, from which the soldier's title was supposedly derived (French *dragon*, carbine, implying fire-breathing). At first it was the practice to take horse holders with each troop, but by the Civil War period one man in ten was detailed to do this duty when his comrades dismounted to go into action. In most regiments at that time, dragoons were the army's handymen. They did escort duty, and carried forward *fascines* (bundles of wood) to fill up trenches in the line of advance, and to hedge in batteries.

One of the effects of the Civil War was to sicken the public of war. Factious divisions in families and between friends created widespread discontent, and the to-and-fro movements of the contending armies stripped the countryside of supplies over and over again. Food shortage was common, for farmers became tired of raising sale crops to be trodden down, so they grew simply for themselves. This check on agriculture endured long after the war; in some parts of Devonshire it was unusual to see an acre or two of wheat, even in 1675.

The years of war demonstrated that the army system was still defective. Food supplies for the troops and fodder for the horses still depended upon haphazard arrangements for "living off the country" as in the Middle Ages. Though stoppages were made for equipment issues, there was no general provision of clothing, which led to quiet pillaging of the country people's hedge-drying linen. Sometimes actual commandeering was done by both sides, so that the bolder civilian was disposed to defend his property against any soldier.

Billeting and sanitation were everpresent problems. In winter the military activities dwindled through sheer necessity, for open bivouacs in bad weather took too great a toll of men and clothing, and tent camps were most uncommon. Even an ordinary cold can much impair a man's mental processes and physical activity, so a commander's mind was well occupied in trying to safeguard his unit.

10. Continental Developments

When Parliamentary forces had gained victory, and the King had been executed, Parliament found that it had created its own master. The power of Cromwell and his army brought about the rule of the soldier, even to the extent of musketeers entering the House to enforce their leader's demands. He, the former country gentleman, had become first the dogged, inflexible soldier, then the symbol of inexorable will. From this period of army rule dated the public antipathy that was shown to the professional soldier for centuries afterward.

[120]

Oliver Cromwell died in 1658, and in the resultant confusion another forceful army figure loomed large. George Monk, of Potheridge in north Devon, commanded a regiment of foot stationed in Scotland. As part of a political move to bring to the throne Charles Stuart, son of the dead king, he brought his regiment south after crossing the Tweed at Coldstream. He entered London in February, 1660, and he was a prime mover in the Restoration, by which Charles II reached London in May. Monk's regiment was then renamed the Coldstream Regiment of Foot Guards.

One of the most significant ceremonies of the Restoration was the creation of the first true standing army from units of both Royalist and Parliamentarian troops. On February 14th, 1661, the "Lord General's Regiment of Foot, and Life Guard of Horse" laid down their arms on Tower Hill, to signify disbandment, and took up their arms again in the King's service.

Charles II raised three troops of Life Guards from among his Royalist fellow exiles. The units wore different facings, and were first known as the King's, the Queen's, and the Duke of York's respectively. At the same time the Earl of Oxford formed the Royal Horse Guards (the Blues)—eight troops, one consisting of eighty men, and the others of sixty each. These men were formerly troopers in Colonel Unton Crooke's regiment of the New Model Army. In the picture are shown soldiers of the King's Life Guards and the Royal Horse Guards, as they were in 1663. The "Household Cavalry" (the collective name) paraded with cuirasses, swords, pistols, and carbines. Their headgear was at first plumed hats, then steel caps, and finally iron-lined caps, and they wore loose blue cloaks with small capes as weather protection.

From the date of their inception, the Household cavalry regiments and Foot Guards were the cream of the British forces. The most decorative in peacetime and the most effective in action, they demonstrated the true pattern of the soldier.

HOUSEHOLD CAVALRY, 1663.

Another service came into prominence soon after these units were formed. For some time before, soldiers had been occasionally drafted for duty on board ship, but after the Restoration battalions of Marines were raised for the purpose. Possibly they were recruited from London-trained bands, as the Royal Marines have always enjoyed the privilege of marching through the city with fixed bayonets and colours.

Marines of the present day refute the title of "soldier,"

for they rightly consider their great service as a separate entity. However, the original Royal Marines were soldiers, and the 1st Foot Guards (later the Grenadier Guards) served as Marines soon after their formation in 1661.

Three years later, there was raised "The Lord High Admiral's Regiment of Foot," the last phrase being changed in 1684 to "Maritime Regiment." The uniform was yellow with red facings, grey breeches, and long red stockings. Flintlock muskets and swords were the issued arms, and the officers had orders to give the men frequent drill at the "great guns" on board ship.

[123]

These permanent forces of 17th-century England were a development of the basic French system that had evolved at the end of the Middle Ages. Louis XI (1461–83) had begun the move by calling on 20,000 seasoned troops as regulars, to garrison towns along the Somme. He called the companies "Picardy Bands," and Francis I subsequently raised "Bands of Champagne." Early in the 17th century, Louis XIII (1610–43) made a contribution with "Bands of Piedmont," whose troops comprised Gascons, Provençals, Basques, and Corsicans.

Picardy and Champagne troops, hailing from the north, were solid, tough, dependable soldiers, while the Piedmont men were mercurial and adaptable. This difference in character between armies of the Rhine and those of Italy persisted through the story of the French soldier.

When the French authorities conquered their fear of putting a compact, organized force under the control of one man, regiments were formed; Louis XIII had thirty regiments. Artillery was well disposed in a corps that was supported by successive kings.

In recruiting additional troops, each colonel was responsible for his own activities. Usually the choice was made among men of no trade, adventurers, and ne'er-do-wells. Any methods from persuasion to intimidation were permissible, and a great number of foreign troops, chiefly Germans, were employed. Louis XIV (1643–1715) would not permit the term "French army" to be used—it was the "army of France," consisting of almost fifty per cent aliens. The view was that a foreign soldier was in effect three men—one less to be an enemy, one man in the fighting line, and one Frenchman saved from leaving his work. This defective system produced a field army of mercenaries and pressed Frenchmen.

Regional militia provided a background force whose men did garrison duty, and who were employed as guards and escorts. A distinguished form of service for the younger sons of gentlemen was found in the King's Musketeers, or in the Guards of Cardinal Richelieu, the King's chief minister.

Though the feudal system had declined, the old seigneur and peasant relationship still remained. Richelieu wished to break the power of the nobles by making them dependents of the king, so a number of young nobles were given army commissions. In this way, officer strength became so great that some companies numbered only thirty men. However, such an arrangement gave extreme flexibility in movement.

Cardinal Richelieu's statesmanship was exerted to the full when the greatest Continental war to that date was being fought out. The Thirty Years' War (1618–48) was a gigantic struggle between Protestant nations and the powerful Catholic League. In Germany, the Protestant armies had been shattered by the Catholics of Austria, their forces led by the outstanding general Count Tilly of Brabant and his second in command Adalbert von Wallenstein of Bohemia (present-day Czechoslovakia). Both these remarkable soldiers were completely ruthless, Tilly in particular being devoid of humanity and regardless of anything but his objective. He and Wallenstein permitted the most frightful atrocities in captured German cities.

Denmark surrendered to the troops of the Austrian Empire in 1629, but soon afterwards Wallenstein was temporarily retired, under suspicion of double-dealing. It was an unfortunate move for the Empire. Cardinal Richelieu wished to break the Austrian power before it threatened France. He had been mediator for a soldier-king in the north—Gustavus Adolphus of Sweden (1594–1632)—in concluding a peace between Poland and Sweden.

Richelieu persuaded the Swedish king to take the

Protestants' part in the southern struggle, and none was better fitted. The King's recruiting system was based on the old assize of arms, which covered men's lives from youth to age. However, he excused certain industries altogether, and took only a tenth of the other workers who had settled homes and work.

In the army, energetic reforms had been effected on weapon-training and tactics. Both pikes and muskets were relatively light in weight, the pikes only eleven feet long, and the muskets manageable without rests. Constant drill had produced musketeers capable of firing at a rate of thirty shots per hour, and the King's artillerymen were of equal standard. Light guns were the speciality—4-pounder infantry guns, 2-pounder swivel breech-loaders, and even leather guns. The latter were devised by Sir Alexander Hamilton, a Scottish artillerist. His countrymen, fighting as valued mercenaries in the Scots Brigade, called the guns "Sandy's stoups." Actually, the leather was bound and lined with tin.

When the Swedes were in action against Tilly, their dispositions were in complete contrast to the Imperial army. Tilly employed a formation like that of a hundred years before. Huge, solid masses of pikemen were flanked by files of musketeers, while the Swedish infantry were alternated in small detachments of pikes and shot, for mutual cover. These units were only three ranks deep, with a fire order drill in ranks for the shot.

In all the Swedish king's dispositions we see the urge for flexible units. His cavalry were not bunched in heavy masses, but spread in detachments strong enough to hit hard without clumsiness. The other outstanding characteristic of the whole army was superb discipline, resulting in skilful handling of arms—one account of the battle of Lützen (1632) says that the Swedish guns fired three shots to one from the Austrians.

Arms training, discipline, sound tactics—excellent attributes for an army, and the Swedes added to them another of great worth. At first the German citizens were not altogether welcoming to the foreign army. When they saw the sensible, orderly conduct of the soldiers, in such contrast to the barbarism of the Imperial army, their confidence was gained. Ruffianism and robbery were unknown, and twice a day the Swedes assembled around their regimental chaplains for prayer. Europe had never seen such an army, nor such dogged endurance that kept the field in summer and winter.

None of the three great soldiers of the Thirty Years' War saw the peace that concluded it at Westphalia. Gustavus was shot at Lützen, Tilly died of wounds at almost the same time, and Wallenstein was murdered for his ambitions in 1634. Germany, the scene of the conflict, had been cruelly devastated. Of those armies that had operated there, only the Swedes and their allies had been true soldiers; most of the others had been plunder-mad adventurers and brutes. At least half the population of 20,000,000 had died in one way or another, many towns and villages were ashes, and huge tracts of country were like deserts. Germany's famous combine of trading cities, the Hanseatic League, broke up in 1635, funds exhausted, and the whole country lay in a torpor for many years.

The war had been fought out with conventional arms, but two relatively new weapons were developed on the Continent during the 17th century, one being the hand grenade. La Mark Du Bellay, the French historian, recorded that large numbers of grenades were made at Arles in 1536, and that the Comte de Rendan was killed by one at the siege of Rouen in 1562. "Grenade" derived from the Spanish *granada*, pomegranate, with reference to the missile's shape.

[127]

These grenades were of simple form—hollow cast-iron globes a few inches in diameter. They contained two or three ounces of powder, and each had a short fuse, to be lighted before throwing.

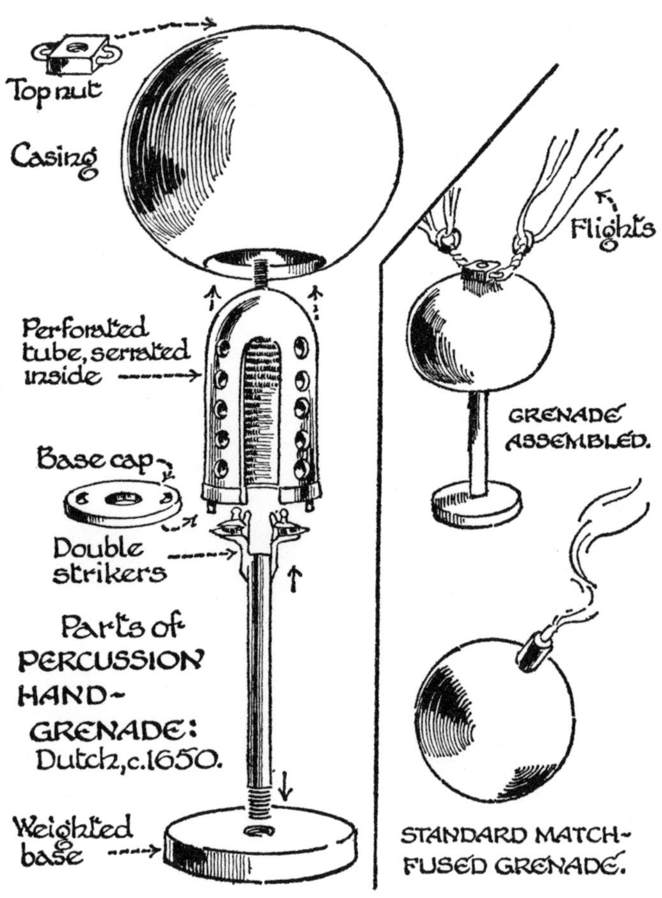

Through the use of this weapon arose a new type of soldier, the grenadier. In 1667, four or five grenadiers were attached to each company of French infantry, for instance, and three years later separate companies were formed. Their equipment included a *fusil* (a light flintlock musket)

[128]

with a sling for putting the weapon on their shoulders before throwing a grenade, a pouch of grenades, and a slow match in a case. Grenadiers were chosen from tall, strong men with long limbs, who could gain the utmost range.

GRENADIER, 1678.

Very soon English military authorities followed suit. John Evelyn, the diarist, wrote that he saw at the Hounslow camp soldiers called "granadiers, who were dexterous in flinging hand grenades" (June 29th, 1678). A picture of the grenadier is shown. He had buff crossbelts over his red

[129]

coat, and a waistbelt with a frog at the left front. The tufted buttonloops on the coat were probably the origin of the "louped clothes" in the song, *The British Grenadiers*. A baggy crown hung down the back of the furred cap, which crown was later stiffened upright to form the mitre cap of the 18th-century soldier. Only grenadiers and fusiliers were permitted to wear the mitre cap; both units had slings on their firelocks, as their weapons were called in the British army, and the three-cornered hat would not have let the sling pass. Grenadiers, of course, slung their muskets to throw the grenade, and fusiliers used their slings when called upon to heave at a gun wheel in soft going. Included with the grenadier's kit was a hammer-backed hatchet, a sword, and a pouch of grenades.

Standard grenades were ignited by a quick match type of fuse, but the Dutch grenade of c.1650 that appears in our picture was apparently the first percussion pattern. It contained a perforated tube with a serrated interior. A double or single flint striker was fixed to a rod which fitted into the tube, and the lower end of the rod was screwed into a weighted base. Flights at the top of the grenade, and the weight of the base, kept it steady when thrown, so that the base was first to strike. This drove the striker head up the tube, creating sparks which passed through the perforations to the bursting charge.

The grenade was a newly-developed missile weapon, which could be projected from a bell-shaped cup fixed to the muzzle of a musket, but a close-quarters arm was the second of the new innovations. Bayonets were originally used by 16th-century German hunters, but the first form of military bayonet appeared in France about 1640–50. As then issued, it was described as a dagger when mentioned in drill books, and it was stuck by its tapered grip into the musket muzzle. A soldier carried his bayonet in the waistbelt frog at the left front.

[130]

Many difficulties attended the use of the early bayonet, but with the introduction of a practical form of socket the musket and bayonet provided a complete offensive and defensive unit for one man. Through this development the old pike and shot combination was outdated before the end of the 17th century.

In spite of the desolation created by the war in Germany, it was there that the greatest European military development took place. It began in the new kingdom of Prussia, where Frederick William (born 1688, died 1740) was indulging his passion for army organization. He was greatly indebted to Field Marshal Prince Leopold of Dessau (1676–1747) whose drill book and military science formed the background of the Prussian army. Leopold made two particular innovations—the iron ramrod to replace wood, and the uniform marching step, which helped immensely in taking the men over long distances without undue fatigue.

The King only engaged in one war, an alliance against Sweden in 1715, but he devoted his whole life to equipping and drilling his army. It was expanded from 48,000 men to 83,500, the best-trained force in Europe. Frederick regarded the army as one might a group of toy soldiers. He went as far as to collect a special unit of giants, the Potsdam Guard. These men were brought in from all over Europe—kidnapped, in some cases.

This basic militarism was enormously expanded by the king's son and successor, Frederick II, "the Great," who reigned from 1740 to 1786. The Potsdam Guard, 2,000 strong, was still maintained "of great stature and comliness, well cloathed, and distinguished by silver-laced hats and black cockades."

In the line regiments, short, close fitting blue coats were worn, with heart-shaped elbow patches of leather. White breeches were issued, of wool or linen according to the season, and with them black spatterdashes (gaiters). These had been white under the old king, but the men tended to put them on with pipe-clay still damp upon them, which caused rheumatism.

Prussian soldiers were always clean and neat, with carefully powdered pigtails. An ordinary infantryman's pay was eight *groschen* a week (about 1s. 2d.), which seems low compared with other armies. He had to pay threepence for washing and weapon-cleaning materials, but he received an allowance of bread.

Every householder in the towns had one or two soldiers billeted. Other countries, including England, were developing the Spanish idea of barracks. These were originally slave compounds (*baraques*) in Spanish America. The Prussian system, reported by an English observer in 1779, was devised to keep soldiers in close, friendly contact with citizens, so that the army should not appear to be a separate entity. In England, remarked the observer, it might not have been advisable to provide barracks in case a body of men concerted mutiny there!

An impressive exercise, called a review, was seen by the Englishman at Potsdam, where 36,000 men took part, under the King's direction. It occupied seven hours, and featured skilled, tactical use of the three arms, with tremendous discharges of blank cartridge. A remarkable feature was the rapid-fire, while advancing, produced from 9-pounder field-guns.

Cavalry charges were made at full gallop, though the men kept precisely spaced; even hussars charged home like heavy cavalry. The cuirassiers were the cream of the horse troops, wearing buffcoats and musketproof breastplates. As a psychological feature, the infantry were trained to shout as they advanced to the attack, and the effect was enhanced by a number of drummers.

This perfection of movement was produced by iron

discipline from top to bottom of the command. A recruit newly brought in was treated kindly for his early instruction. Later, if he was not as smart as he should have been, vigorous caning was given.

It was unpardonable to move an eyelid on parade, and kit and arms had to be speckless. Any deficiency in men or officers was attributed to slackness in the next stage up, so everyone was constantly at his peak. Officers developed a staid, thoughtful, unrelaxing air, and the men became literally unthinking machines. Desertion was almost impossible. There was a large reward for the peasant who seized a deserter, and a heavy penalty for sheltering one.

With these features—superlative training and top-grade flintlock arms and cannon—Frederick's army became the model for Europe. During the Seven Years' War (1756–1763), his epic struggle against the combined forces of Austria, France, Russia, Saxony, and Sweden, gained for Prussia an important place among European nations.

11. Russian and British Army Service

Russia's part in the Seven Years' War was brought to an end by the death of the Tsarina Elizabeth in 1761. The Russian army was a considerable factor at that time, but it had only been developed during the previous seventy years. Until the 17th century it was a motley collection of ignorant, downtrodden peasants, raised by the great landed proprietors on a feudal basis. During the horrors of the Tartar invasion, in the early Middle Ages, the Russians first learned the value of concerted resistance.

Though Ivan IV raised some arquebusiers on a per-

manent footing about 1550, the first definite establishment
was the corps of Streltsy, the royal bodyguard of the mid-
17th century. Contemporary pictures show them in full-
skirted coats with heavily-braided buttonholes, long boots,
and curious round hats, like turbans. These brawny,

RUSSIAN STANDING ARMY—EARLY STAGES.

bearded soldiers were a source of disturbance; they were
often in revolt over some alleged injustice.

A great reorganization of the ill-found army was carried
out by Peter I, "the Great" (1682–1725). While in action
against the Turks in 1695, he realized a number of essential needs in his army, such as a supreme commander to
co-ordinate effort, and skilled engineers to smooth the path
of the army. For his own part, he studied gunnery at

[135]

Konigsberg and Pilau, gaining a Master of Artillery certificate.

In the Tsar's preparations for war against Sweden he called for freeman volunteers, instead of bringing out the feudal levies. He offered eleven roubles a year (then about 22s.), with food and drink provided. This undertaking was a great success; within three months twenty-nine new regiments, 32,000 men, were armed and partly trained. Regimental commanders were foreigners, but all other officers were Russian.

At length Peter's new army numbered thirty-five regiments, composed of men whose sole interest was the army —no reluctant transplanted tradesmen among them. A German-style uniform was adopted, with dark green coats and small, black, three-cornered hats. There was a single shoulder belt supporting the cartridge pouch on the right, and each infantryman had a musket and bayonet, but no sword.

Peter spared no effort in the technicalities of military training, but the fighting spirit had not developed. His first action with Swedish troops ended in disaster. The ammunition supplies failed, and he was outwitted in a snowstorm, losing four men for every Swedish soldier lost. A later engagement resulted in the rout of 27,000 Russian troops, the four reserve regiments having fled at the first shots. When the tide turned, the army still showed itself as immature; after a victory at Narva, in 1704, the Tsar's troops fell to shooting down the civilian population. It is said that the Tsar, in checking the outbreak, personally cut off the head of a disobedient soldier.

Within a year of that event, Peter disposed 40,000 infantry and 20,000 cavalry, the majority being seasoned troops who had been in action several times. His arms and munition supplies were of good quality and well maintained. Where the cavalry had formerly carried only swords and lances, they were armed with carbines and pistols. In the artillery, the pieces were standardized, and his 3-pounder infantry guns took the field with mounted gunners.

Between 1705 and 1709, a recruiting system was developed whereby each community furnished one recruit for every twenty taxable households. Groups of 500 to 1,000 were mustered in their nearest towns, and housed and trained in barracks, where invalided officers and sergeants served as instructors. When evasions were attempted, the Tsar ordered that defaulters should be replaced by the local community, so the practice ceased.

In 1707, there was a rebellion among the populace, aggrieved by the demands of the service in manpower and work on forts. However, the disturbance was effectively crushed by the army. Shortly afterwards, the troops put up a gallant fight against a Swedish invasion by Charles XII, and gained final victory at Poltava in 1708.

Russian forces included a valuable contingent from the eastern territories, notably the Cossacks. These fiery horsemen figured in a mid-18th century account by an itinerant German pastor. The Don Cossacks, regular troops of fierce aspect, were fitted out with blue jackets, very wide blue breeches, and red Polish coats with open sleeves. On their shaven heads they wore small red caps, and they had close half boots. Irregular Cossacks wore an all-blue uniform.

Each man's arms comprised a fifteen-foot lance resting in a leather sling, three pistols, a musketoon (short, wide-bored firearm), a sabre, and a long knife. In addition he carried a cutting whip, the *kourbash*. Irregular Cossacks received no pay; they lived by plunder.

Other semi-barbarian troops of horse were the blue-clad Kalmuks, mounted archers of extraordinary skill, who were supposedly accurate to 200 yards, and Carcolpaks, in grey. The latter were armed like the Cossacks.

While these developments were taking place in Europe, British forces were being placed on a more permanent footing. Between 1661 and 1692 nearly fifty regiments were taken into the British service—cavalry, dragoons, fusiliers, and line regiments of particular counties. Service was for life or until a man was invalided out to beg his bread; there was no general provision for an old soldier's welfare. Kilmainham Hospital (1680) and Chelsea (1681) were the first institutions for such a service, but the intake was limited. For this reason, a large proportion of professional soldiers were men who could find no other livelihood, or who were avoiding the law.

The Duke of Schomberg, commenting on an English garrison in Ireland, said that those new recruits who had matchlocks were most uncertain about fixing the lighted match into the cleft in the cock. However, a sweeping reform of William III of Orange (1688–1702) rearmed British forces with flintlocks, and pikes were finally withdrawn in 1704.

Early in the 18th century, the newly-equipped British army saw action in France under John Churchill (1650–1722), the famous Duke of Marlborough.

Though he was a double-dealer with his superiors, the Duke was devoted to the army's welfare. His great concerns were adequate feeding, good kit, and reliable arms and munitions. Pay as regularly issued, and discipline was strict. The cavalry were equipped with breastplates but no backplates, and no pistol ammunition was permitted, except for horse line guards—the men charged with the sword alone. When the infantry had musket drill, wood or bone "snappers" were substituted for flints, to save the latter for actual firing.

An infantry battalion in action was drawn up in three

[138]

ranks, with grenadiers at the flanks, and the colonel in front with the leading drummer. Loading and firing was done by drum signal, but the two centre platoons held their fire, as the colonel and drummer stood before them. When the remaining platoons had fired, the colonel and his drummer stepped aside, the centre platoons fired, and the two men returned before them again.

Marlborough was not a brilliant general, but he had the invaluable quality of affinity with the men—he was a soldier with them. A story is told of a group of infantrymen who were aggrieved over the coarse quality of issue shirts. They threw a number of shirts into the Duke's garden, and, after investigation, he amended the matter without punishing the soldiers. An Army Clothing Order of 1708 detailed as the issue a well-lined coat, to serve as a waistcoat in the second year, a waistcoat, kersey breeches and strong stockings and shoes, two good shirts, two neckcloths, and "a good strong hat, well laced."

In Marlborough's army, the artillery had no official standing. A unit consisted of a master gunner, two master gunner's mates, thirty-two gunners, and thirty-two *matrosses*, who looked after the tackle. Attached to the artillery train were pioneers for constructing emplacements, a drummer on a special carriage, and a mortar crew commanded by a *petardier* (a petard was a portable mine). The mortars were of cast iron and the field guns of brass.

Civil drivers were still employed, and a fusilier escort protected them and the guns. Aprons were issued to the escorts, who were expected to help along the guns in boggy ground.

Through departmental bungling, no artillery train was available for action against the Jacobite rebels of 1715, so in the following year four permanent companies of artillery were proposed. Two were raised at the outset, with nine officers and ninety-two men in each, but in 1727 the total was increased to four companies. In that year was created the title that was to earn undying fame—the Royal Regiment of Artillery.

As before, the gunners were controlled by the Board of Ordnance, and civilian drivers were employed until the raising of the Royal Horse Artillery in 1793. The artillery service was unique. No flags were flown by the unit, for the guns were its colours. Its twin mottoes *Quo fas et gloria ducunt*, "Where fame and glory lead," and *Ubique*, "Everywhere," were amply borne out by its subsequent history.

After Marlborough's retirement, the Army declined for a time. Its numbers fell, and a great proportion of the recruits were low ruffians, who brought discredit upon the name of soldier. Severe discipline did a great deal to remedy this; lashes were administered by the hundred, a practice which earned the British soldier the name of "Bloody-back." Convicted deserters were shot by a selected party, carefully briefed by a sergeant. A reserve firing squad waited in the rear, in case the first party failed to kill.

Desertion was sometimes the soldier's refuge from appalling debt. Each regiment was a business concern, run by the colonel and the adjutant. Kit was issued to the men, and their pay was cut by "stoppage money" to keep up the payments incurred for kit and other items. For instance, in 1720 a sergeant of horse was paid 15s. 9d. a week. Stoppages and his horse's keep cost him 8s. 9d., so he had 7s. for himself. A sergeant of foot, with 7s. in pay and 6s. deduction, had only 1s. left. Dragoons received 9s. 11d., with 8s. 9d. in stoppages, leaving 1s. 2d. It would seem that the ordinary infantryman was still the poorest soldier, with 3s. 6d. a week. Deductions left only 6d., a state of affairs that endured until 1797.

[140]

This situation led to desertion, for if some loss or break-age occurred, the foot-soldier, in particular, might find his debt impossible to pay. For instance, if he lost his musket, he was fined 30s., with a further 5s. if the bayonet was lost.

23RD FOOT, 1745
(LATER ROYAL WELCH FUSILIERS).

That would mean about sixteen months without any pay at all, while begging for his food.

A regimental fund called *overmoney* provided shoes, stockings, and gaiters, such equipment as was shared, physic, arms repairs, and a yearly fee of 2s. for a surgeon. Sometimes a recruit of independent means would join the ranks as an ordinary soldier, and would supply his own equipment. He would be known as a *private* soldier, i.e., privately equipped. Occasionally the term was *private centinel*, referring to early 100-strong companies. When the practice declined, the title *private* was applied to any infantryman without other rank.

Gunner, Royal Artillery, 1742   Engineer and Artificer, 1759.

Some attention was paid to the ordinary soldier's hair style at the beginning of the new century. Previously the soldier had worn his hair as he pleased, but the civilian fashion of powdered wigs was reflected in the infantry, in particular. Officers wore actual wigs, but other ranks had their hair tied back at first; then a pigtail was decreed, and this endured until the end of the century. In imitation of

[142]

civilian hair powder, the men's hair was treated with candle-grease and flour.

When the army had regained its former strength and status, in the middle of the 18th century, a number of specialist units were formed. For instance, in 1756 a light troop was added to each regiment of dragoons. These light dragoons were styled *hussars* in 1758, after the Hungarian light cavalry of that name. The dragoons were armed with carbines and pistols of similar bore, bayonets, and light, straight swords. There was an issue of canvas covers for gunlocks. Slings for the carbine were attached to the light-weight saddle, and the horses were of hunter type.

Where other troops had revers to their coats, the light dragoons were not thus fitted out, and the helmet was a special close pattern of boiled leather, mounted with brass. Like all mounted troops, the dragoons wore eight-inch strips of white canvas, called *boot-stockings*, buttoned around their knees to protect their breeches from boot-blacking.

The men were given special training in horsemanship, and in firing from the saddle, but no exercises in reconnaissance, their true function. However, we can see that dragoons were no longer mounted infantry, in that they fired from the saddle.

Another light unit was the company of 550 infantrymen specially equipped by General James Wolfe (1727–59) for his campaign in Canada. Small, active men who were proven marksmen formed this volunteer detachment. An effort was made to reduce their impedimenta, and to make the kit suitable for fighting in woods. A close-fitting blue or green jacket was issued, with drawers of the same shade, a close peaked cap, and a black bearskin ruff.

The knapsack was braced high on the shoulders, with the cloth-covered *canteen* (water bottle) below it, and a tomahawk was slung in a case at the right hip. Seventy

[143]

rounds were carried, fifty in the cartouche box slung under the left arm, and the rest in special breast pockets, with spare flints. Under the right arm a powder horn was slung on a webbing strap. An interesting point of camouflage

LIGHT INFANTRY, 1758.

was the growing of a beard, or the use of smut, to cover the face as much as possible.

While light infantry were the smallest men of the foot, at the other end of the scale were the grenadiers, who were chosen from the tallest. For the latter, the equipment was heavy for that period. When on the march, the grenadier

[144]

carried his rolled topcoat upon his knapsack. This was slung around his shoulders, and it contained two shirts, two stocks, two pairs of stockings, a pair of summer breeches, a pair of shoes, brushes, a ball of bootblacking, and six days' rations. A grey canvas haversack hung at his left side, and in addition he had his canteen, sword, bayonet, musket with sling, and ammunition, the total weight being nearly seventy pounds.

Though the 18th-century uniform coat was full-skirted, the skirts were looped back on each side to free the legs for marching. White, pipe-clayed gaiters were worn during the first half of the century, but, as in the Prussian army, the men contracted rheumatism through putting the gaiters on while they were wet. While they were in camp, the troops were in six-man ridge pole tents, with a big three-foot camp kettle to each tent. Arms were stored in bell tents called bells of arms, with the regimental crests on the tents.

A practical step forward was made when the unorganized pioneer service was brought under better control. In 1741, a School of Military Engineering was established, and sixteen years later the first commissions were granted to students of the school. All engineers were officers at the outset, and small local bodies of pioneers were raised as required, with artificers appointed from among them as noncommissioned officers. A century of gallant service to their brother warriors gained the unit the title of "Royal Engineers" in 1855. Their original officer status was recalled by the ceremonious form of address on parade, "Gentlemen of the Royal Engineers. . . ."

In the story of the British soldier, the record of the Scotsman in the army is outstanding. Once the bitter enemy of the English Crown, he became its loyal supporter. Highlanders in particular were deadly enemies of the

English for long after the union of the two Crowns. Bad English administration and fierce Highland pride shed much blood on either side. It was wisely said that the Highlander was then a great fighter but a poor soldier. Organization and discipline were hotly resented. This, combined with bitter clan rivalry, made military service difficult.

"Free companies" of Highlanders at length accepted service with locally-stationed English detachments, each body to be attached to the force until the latter left the district. This practice began in 1693. Highland dress was worn by the recruits—the belted plaid (*Breacan-a-fheilidh* in Gaelic), which was cloak and kilt in one, twelve yards of double-width material. When the plaid was put on, the belt was laid on the ground, and the plaid was spread with its central part over the belt. There were pleats in the part lying across the belt, but part of each end was left unpleated. The wearer lay upon the plaid and fastened the belt around his waist. This permitted the lower part to be arranged as a kilt, while the upper half served as a cloak; this was looped up to the left shoulder.

There were no uniform clan tartans at that time; the basic sett or pattern was dark green and black, and it was not until 1822 that clan tartans were devised, for the coronation visit of George IV.

Those Scottish companies of 1693 were heavily armed. They had regulation firelocks in addition to the normal Highland gentleman's equipment of broadsword, target with spike, steel pistols, dirk, and *skene dhu* (black knife) worn in the stocking top. Civilians were forbidden to carry arms, however, so many young men joined the Highland companies to be able to do this. Enlisted men in the regular Scottish army establishment wore "hodden grey," as their service was separate from the English Army until the Union of 1707.

[146]

In 1739, the free companies were united into "The Highland Regiment of Foot," the 43rd. Later, the title was changed to the 42nd, the Royal Highland Regiment. The regiment was known later in the century as *Am*

THE HIGHLAND REGIMENT, 1739.

Freiceadan Dubh, the Black Watch, though the title did not become official until 1861. It may have been an opprobrious nickname applied by anti-English Scots. However, it became synonymous with all that makes a soldier.

[147]

12. The American Soldier

While the British Army was developing its various branches, a similar move was being made in the New World. Those subjects of the King who were called Americans, English-speaking descendants of former settlers, raised troops to maintain their struggle with the American Indians and with the French settlers.

British Government records and contemporary journals give details of units raised by different states and cities. There is mention of the New York City Cavalry of 1724, and details of an infantry regiment to be raised in

Pennsylvania by March 1759, for the duration of the French war in Canada. A noticeable point regarding infantry is that the pay of a "Private Man" was 3s. a day (New York currency), about 43 cents, and that of a lieutenant 6s.

Not all Indians were hostile, though unwise treatment often caused enmity. In 1761, the Royal Magazine published a speech of loyalty by a Messaga chief, and the London Magazine reported the presentation at Court of a chief of the Cherokees.

When the colossal mismanagement of the Government had infuriated the Americans, the British regulars serving in America were in a delicate position. General Gage, commanding, issued orders that the men should not retaliate if insulted or even struck, but that no man should leave his quarters unarmed. Gage had 16,000 men all told —too small a force to quell a rebellious population. Shouts of "Bloody-back" and offensive missiles greeted the troops in the street, and some loyal Americans were tarred and feathered.

Before the outbreak at Lexington, in 1775, the colonists had been openly making hostile preparations. Companies of *minutemen* were being armed and drilled; their title meant that they were on call at a minute's notice. A number of the local bodies of troops declared for the King when fighting began, and they did valuable service, but the great majority of the Americans united to "hit the British." The Declaration of Independence, on July 4th, 1776, crystallized their animosity into a revolution.

The most important symbol of the subsequent war was the rifle. Americans of the woods and plains were highly skilled in its use, and American industry had made a feature of its production for many years. It would seem that rifle manufacture was much more widespread in America than in Britain. Swiss and German gunsmiths in

AMERICAN RIFLEMEN, 1776~83
Based on contemporary prints.

Pennsylvania had developed the so-called Kentucky rifle about 1725, and it was highly popular among countrymen.

In Europe, rifle-armed troops were very much in the minority. The 60th Foot (later the King's Royal Rifle Corps) was an early British rifle unit in 1755, and German

Length c. 6ft: bore varied.

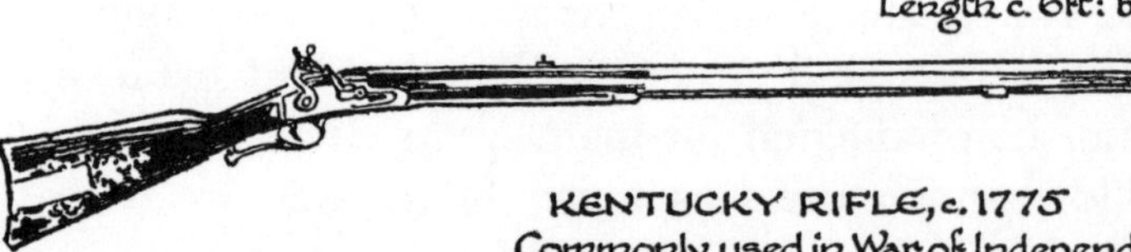

KENTUCKY RIFLE, c. 1775
Commonly used in War of Independence.

jägers (huntsmen) were later formed into similar bodies. In fact, the bugle horn badge of present-day light infantry regiments refers to the huntsman origin of rifle corps.

Rifle superiority was fatally demonstrated on April 18th, 1775, when the skirmish between musket-armed British troops and Americans took place at Lexington. There is controversy as to who fired the first shots, but in the running fight that followed the red-coated British were badly hit. Over 250 men were killed, wounded, or missing when the action closed, while the opponents lost only sixty. Skilful advance under cover, and accurate shooting, gave the Americans their advantage.

When the American hero George Washington (1732–1799) took command of the colonists' motley forces, it was an unenviable task. His army consisted of ill-assorted militia, in every variety of dress, and short of every provision. Illiteracy was the rule, and it was terribly difficult to show the men a reason for obedience to orders. Their minds were a welter of confused ideas—vague notions on national liberty mixed with obstinacy over personal freedom.

Washington had seen a great deal of service in the French and Indian war of 1753–58, and he had been commander of the Virginian forces. In his army of 1775, supplies were a nightmare. At the highest estimate, there were not thirty rounds per man, nothing for artillery, and not a hundred pounds of powder for sale in all the thirteen states.

As the men's rifles varied in bore, taking bullets which ranged from thirteen to thirty to the pound of lead, each man cast his own bullets. By the enlistment order, each man was directed to bring a good firearm, a cartouche box, a blanket, and a knapsack. Equipment was slung on crossbelts over the ordinary clothes.

An example of shooting standards was displayed in a

woodsmen's exhibition arranged by Washington, wherein riflemen hit a pole nearly every time at 250 yards. Shooting was second nature to the colonists, but it was hard to persuade them into the heavy work of artillery service.

At the outset, Washington's forces were the most unlikely soldier material. Discipline was anathema; the men went home in a huff at the slightest suggestion of interference with their liberty. When their covenanted three months of duty had elapsed, nothing would keep them from leaving the army.

The officers were of thoroughly bad type, either foolishly familiar with the men, or brutally severe. Any popular man could become a captain if he could gather enough men to form a company, and a citizen who could collect enough for a regiment was made a colonel. Other officers were elected by the privates.

In the camps, conditions were vile, through the men's neglect of personal cleanliness and communal hygiene. Dead horses lay in or near the camps, heaps of offal stood unburied, and sewage ran among the huts. A wrangling group of doctors formed the medical unit, and the hospitals were mere bedless pestholes.

As long as the authorities respected their undertakings, the conditions of service were far preferable to those in the British Army. For instance, a private in the Massachusetts Militia was paid $36 per lunar month. His daily rations were a pound of bread, at least a pound of meat, a pint of milk, a quart of beer, and a small quantity of vegetables. Once a week salt fish was available instead of meat, and there was a weekly ration of six ounces of butter and a pound of soap between six men.

Washington's constant efforts were directed to improving quarters and keeping the army together. Good drafts came from the middle states and Virginia, twelve companies of rifles in all. They comprised men who had enlisted for a year, some having marched 800 miles to join the leader.

These men were exceptional, in view of the constant ebb and flow among the militia. Still, with some longer service at hand, Washington was able to lay the foundations of a continental army. Congress offered a bounty of $20 and a 100 acres of land (to be claimed after the war) for privates who would enlist for the duration.

A general clothing issue of 1776, to be repeated yearly, was listed as two linen hunting shirts, two pairs of overalls (trousers, so called as opposed to breeches and stockings), a sleeved waistcoat, a pair of breeches, two shirts, two pairs of hose, two pairs of shoes, and a hat or a leather cap. Despite these promises, desertion still went on, and Washington's army, hungry, shoeless, and cold, were thoroughly dispirited. Occasionally, when they ran from the British, their commander rode among them and beat them with the flat of his sword, without avail.

In the face of every adversity, Washington kept a force of men under arms. Through the incredible folly of Congress, in December, 1777, the wretched American army went into winter quarters at Valley Forge, Philadelphia, in an appalling state. Smallpox was rampant among them, with their doctors carrying the disease around the rickety huts. Hungry and wasted, the men lacked greatcoats, shoes, even breeches. An account by the Marquis de Lafayette, who brought a French volunteer force to help the colonists, stressed the number of men without coats, shirts, or shoes. In many cases the feet and legs were frozen black and had to be amputated. By February, 1778, nearly 4,000 men were rendered unfit through lack of clothing. They remained crowded in the stinking, chimneyless huts, infested with itch and scurvy.

The slackness of Congress caused the quartermaster general to be exchanged before his successor arrived a week later. Meanwhile, the army starved as the food supplies rotted at the roadside near the depot.

During this period of departmental blundering and near-helplessness, the British commander Lord Howe could have crushed the colonists without the slightest trouble. However, his own indolence and the bumbling Government policy at home condemned the British troops to a "hare and tortoise" situation. Snug in their billets, the army did not press their overwhelming advantage.

In one particular respect, the British raised great animosity. Terms were made with German princes for the hire of mercenary riflemen. For instance, the Prince of Hesse received £6,000 a year for a force of 688 *jägers*. In all 17,000 riflemen were hired, at a cost of £1,500,000.

Both sides were shamefully lax as regards the welfare of prisoners. Americans raged about the six British prison hulks lying offshore, described as black holes of horror; it was alleged that 10,000 Americans had died on the *Jersey* alone. For their own part, with no knowledge or concern about the usages of war, the Americans let their British captives starve, rot, or freeze while not undergoing more positive ill-treatment.

Washington's spirit was unquenchable, but even he must have felt relief when Congress sent him aid in the able person of Frederick von Steuben. This energetic character, from the court of Frederick the Great, was a specialist in the arms manual and in general organization. His first stricture was that the officers did not trouble about the men's welfare, and his first move was to detail the officers in squads to drill under him.

In March, 1778, von Steuben formed a guard of honour for the commander. It was chosen from among the Virginian detachment, fit men of good physique. This group was drilled into a demonstration unit, and the

[154]

manual was the basis for future U.S. Army drill. Loading was carried out in fifteen motions.

There must have been magic in the German's methods. When France allied herself with the colonists, in May,

HESSIAN JÄGER, 1780.

1778, they were able to mount a ceremonial parade and drill display. Ragged they all were, but clean, and almost adequately fed, for at last supplies were getting through. Congress was stirred to make an offer of $10 extra bounty for the duration, with the promise of $80 at the end of the war, and half pay for seven years after that. Very few men actually received the money. In any case, the paper money issued by Congress depreciated so quickly that in two years it was worth only one-twentieth of its face value.

When the reorganization of the army was in full swing, uniformity was the watchword; fire control, postures on parade, a twenty-four-inch step at seventy-five to the minute, suitable for rough going, were all initiated. Marching was done in close column of platoons, to take up the minimum road space and avoid straggling. The camp was precisely laid out in battalions, with cooking and sanitation well arranged, and the men paraded regularly for roll calls and inspections. Congress published in 1779 the Regulations of Valley Forge, the first standard regulations for the US Army. Some of them read quaintly, but the ideas were sound. Captains and lieutenants were adjured to "gain the love of the men."

At that hopeful stage of army development, Congress spoiled all by another fit of insane meanness, disgusting Washington and causing mutiny among the unpaid troops in 1780–81. While at Eutaw Springs, many of General Greene's men were so naked that they padded their equipment straps with moss to ease the chafing. At the taking of Yorktown in 1781, American troops were in French-issued kit, and a great proportion of the men were too naked to leave their tents.

However, through the devotion of their great leader and the Prussian efficiency of von Steuben, the troops were becoming worthy to be called an army. An order of 1782 entreated officers to supervise minutely the men's loading and aiming, while the issue of service stripes and shoulder symbols of rank began in the same year. There was even flour and rendered tallow on issue for the men's hair. Blue uniforms were standardized, with white or red facings according to the type of service.

When the war dragged itself to a close, at the beginning

of 1783, it had proved itself a disgrace to British arms. The most powerful nation in the world had been outwitted by an amateur army. Yet that army was derided by the American civilian. Congress treated the soldiers shamefully by failing all undertakings, and public scorn was poured upon the men as if they were idlers. From this time dates the use of the word "soldiering" to express loafing.

As soon as peace seemed certain, the Congress axe fell upon the army. At one blow it was reduced to 700 men, and almost immediately afterwards to eighty. Only Washington's influence insured an orderly disbanding of that infuriated army. Its commanders proposed a march to take over empty western lands, leaving Congress to negotiate the peace without an army. A further idea was to make Washington king, but he suppressed the whole project, and persuaded the army to break up peaceably.

This great American soldier was justly rewarded with the first Presidency of the United States, a post which he filled nobly without accepting the salary. In 1799, a few days after the President's death, John Marshall expressed public feeling about him in the House of Representatives: "First in war, first in peace, and first in the hearts of his countrymen."

Index